Somerset County Maryland Wills

- 1750-1772 -

I0082474

Compiled by:
Ruth T. Dryden

Southern Historical Press, Inc.
Greenville, South Carolina

Please direct all correspondence and book orders to:
SOUTHERN HISTORICAL PRESS, Inc.
PO Box 1267
Greenville, SC   29602-1267

ISBN #978-1-63914-239-2
Printed in the United States of America

f.1
DIXON,Sarah   5 Feb 1750   14 Feb 1750
    to dau-Sarah
    to sons-Isaac and Thomas
    to-Elizabeth Turpin,Mary Purnell,Thomas Dixon
    to gr.dau-Sarah Purnell
    to-Sarah Purnell d/o Levi
    wit;=Thomas Williams,Ambrose Dixon, Risdon Dixon
    estate to be in the hands of William Turpin until Isaac
        Dixon marries.

f.2-
BEAUCHAMP.Edward   29 Aug 1750   11 Dec 1750
    to wife-Neomy, plantation. exec. after death lands to
    son-Fountain Beauchamp
    to sons-Marcy(exec.), Thomas,John, William, lands
    to-Beauchamp Davis, part tr. LEDBOURN
    to-George Addams, land BUCK RIDGE, he to pay balance due.
    wit;William Turpin,William Willis,John Marridikes

f.2
BOZMAN,Levin   22 Oct 1750   11 Dec 1750
    to brother-Daniel Bozman, dwelling house, ½ lands MORE
        AND CASE IT, WOOLFORDS CHANCE, BOZMANS ADVENTER
    to brother-Phillmon, other ½ afsd.lands
    to sisters-Jane Huitt Bozman,Susannah Bozman
    wit;David Jones, Philemon Jones,John Willin

f.3
LAWS,Robert   8 Apr 1745   21 Mar 1750
    to-son-William, tr. TAYLORS HILL in Dorcester Co. 200a.
    to- John Wallace his dec'd wife's Eleanors part
    to son-Panter Laws, exec.
    wit;Robert Jones,Thomas Jones,Benjamin Jones

f.3
McCLEMMY,William   25 Sep 1750   11 Dec 1750
    to son-Whitty, exec.,dwelling plantation where I live
        (desc.)If no heir to my son William
    toson-Samuel(under 21)
    to daus-Elizabeth King, Sarah Sasser
    wit;Joseph Gillis,William Jones,Benjamin Sasser,John Jones

f.3-4
WOOLFORD,John   7 Mar 1748/9   22 Nov 1750
    towife-Mary, exec., dwelling plantation on e/side of
        Woolford Creek
    to children-Levin (exec.) Betty and Charles
    to son-Charles(under 21) rights to 3 tracts got by my
        wife and Margaret Brown THORN, HACKLALAY, JESIMON (desc.
    to son-Levin, tr. MEADOW at Dam Quarter, tr. in Dorset
        County entailled by his gr.father.
    wit;Joseph McClester, George Hardy,William Allen

WEST,James   6 Nov 1749   9 Mar 1750
    to son-James,plantation where I live
    to wife-Abigail, 1/3rd of manor plant.,GREENS RECANTATION
    200a. on Nanticoke River at mouth of Broad Creek to be sold.
    to-Thomas Byrd guardian of son James. exec.
    wit;Thomas Byrd,Thomas Phillips,Abedengo Green

f.5

RENCHER,Underwood,planter 16 Jan 1750   25 Mar 1750
    to son-William,exec.
    to wife, Sarah,exec., and to all my children
    to dau-Mary
    wit;Charles Dashiell,Charles Ballard,John Dawson

f.5-6

HOPKINS,George of Craven Co. North Carolina
                        20 Jan 1748/9   13 May 1751
    to daus-Judey,Mary,Margaret,Elizabeth,Anne,Hannah, Sarah,
        Alice and Tabitha
    to sons-William,Charles,Steven, Benjamin,Isaac
    to sons-John and George, execs., plantation where I live
        on N/side of NUSS River
    to wife-Elizabeth,exec.
    wit;William Carruthers,Thoms Martin, John Armstrong

f.6

BOZMAN,Anne   29 Sep 1749   26 Mar 1751
    to sister-Bridget Bozman,exec.
    to neice-Eleanor Blewett, exec., and to Martha Blewitt
        d/o Eleanor
    wit;Elenor Covington,Rebecca Covington

f.6

MILLS,William   20 Aug 1749/50   21 Mar 1750
    to cozin-Smith Mills s/o Robert lands where my mother lived
    to son-Samuel
    to gr.sons-Stephen and William Mills plantation where I
        live after their parents decease; the end of plantation
        next to Samuel Handy to Stephen. End next to Noble
        Tull's to William.
    to daus-Isbell Mills exec., Jennett Bevans, Hannah Harvey
    to gr.son-William Smith, Mills Bailey, William Bevans
    to son-Jonathan
    wit;Samuel Handy,Noble Tull, Mary Handy

f.7

DIXON,William   21 Nov 1747   13 May1751
    to wife-Elizabeth, 130a.where I live, plantation 100a.
        of marsh land on Jones Island
    to sons-Risdon, Isaac and David
    to son-Ambrose, 100a marsh on Jones Island, bal.of wife's
        land-after her death.
    to daus-Mary Horsey,Elizabeth Dixon
    to son-Thomas,exec. tr. FIRST CHOICE by Beaver Dam Branch
        212a., 50a. marsh on Jones Island
    wit;George Bozman, George Bozman Jr., William Fordred

WILLIAMS,William,planter   29 Dec 1747   28 Sep 1751
    to wife-Elizabeth, lands BAYBUSH HALL
    to sons-Arthur,Job,John,William
    to daus-Mary,Josebeth,Jemima
    wit;John Roach,Rebecca Roach,Sarah Roach

RIGGIN,John   22 Aug.1747   25 Oct 1751
    to wife-Ann, lands and dwelling house,exec.
    to son-in-law-Robert Dukes
    to-Sabroah Riggin alias Ward, Jonathan Riggin,John Riggin,
        Stephen Riggin,William Riggin,Alce Ward, Rachel Dyes
    wit;John Roach,John Johnson,Thomas Cullin

GILES,William   9 Oct 1749   23 Nov 1751
    to son-Thomas, tr. GILES LOTT
    to son-William, tr.SALLOP 150a., tr. where I live
     PARREMORES FIRST CHOICE 300a., exec.
    Balance to bedivided between all my children
    wit;Daniel Jackson,Edward Bennett,Samuel Jarvis, John
     Williams

CLIFTIN,John   7 Apr 1751   28 Sep 1751
    to wife-Hannah (pregnant),exec.
    to children-Jonathan,George, Machel(eldest son)
    wit;William Edgill,William Evans,William Benston

GIVANS,William   23 Mar 1751   30 Jul 1751
    to father-in-law-William Taylor 100a.,dwelling plantation
    to wife-Ann
    friend,David Kirkpatrick,exec.
    wit;Day Givan,John Badley,Abraham Taylor

HANDY,Elizabeth   3 Apr 1751   6 May 1751
    to sons-William,Samuel,Stephen
    to dau-in-law-Comfort Handy,exec.
    wit;John Davis, Mary Cox,Jonathan Mills

OTLEY,Sarah   3 Apr 1751   1 May 1751
    to-Dorkas Plaverry
    to son-John, exec.
    to three daughters (unnamed)
    wit;John Riggin Sr.,Charles Riggin
    approved by Hannah Clifton,ex.of last will and test. of
     John Clifton

BOSTON,Isaac   30 Apr 1751   28 Sep 1751
    to sons-Isaac,Solomon,Daniel
    tosons-Samuel,Isaac,David,lands on Morumsco Creek(desc.)
    to son-Naboth, land (under 16)
    to daus-Rebecca, Martha,Sarah Boston, Abigail White
    wife-Rachel,plantation where I live,exec.
    Jeffrey Long, Purnell Outten to be appraisers
    Jeffrey Long and Thomas Marshall to be guardians
    wit;Purnell Outten,Lazarus Boston,Esau Boston

BANNISTER,Thomas,planter   19 Aug 1751   2 Nov 1751
    to sons-William (exec.), Charles,plantation, lands (desc.)
    to son-Zekiel,lands on Kings branch WOLF HARBER, CARES
        CHASE, LEW GROUND
    to son-Mitchell
    to daus-Mary Heath,Leah Bannister
    to wife-Sarah,exec.
    to brothers Charles Bannister,Isaac Mitchell, John Robins
        to care for unmarried children
    wit;Joseph Roe,John Roach,James Clark,Abigail Murray

OTTLEY,James,planter   29 Mar 1751   15 Apr 1751
    to wife-Sarah
    to first child born to son James 1/3 pt. ofestate
    to-dau-Naomi Marshall
    to-Mary Ashley
    balance to all my children,(unnamed)
    Col.Robert King,exec.
    wit;Robert Nairne,Ralph Milbourn,Lodowick Milbourn

FENTON,Margaret   13 Dec 1759   22 Dec 1752
    to gr.son-Fenton Catling
    to gr.daus-Ibby Catling,Esther Fenton
    wit;William Dreden,John Haw,John Thompson

DASHIELL,William —   26 Mar 1749   17 Jul 1752
    to eldest son-Robert,dwelling plantation JOHNSONS ADDITION
        174a, tr.GREENWITCH adjoining.
    to 2nd.son Hast, tr. LONG HILL on tipqueen Creek 150a.
    To wife-Sarah, exec.
    to-daus-Elizabeth and Martha(under 16)
    to-Phillip Murray my son-in-law- 1/3pt. of his fathers
        estate which came me by hismother(under 21)
    wit;George Dashiell,Daniel Wailes,Joseph Dashiell

HOPKINS,John Sr.   5 Feb 1752   17 Jul 1752
    to son-Isaac,planat. pt. of CANNONS SHOTT where I live,exec.
    to son-John,exec.,lands, marsh at Cagoes Island
    to gr.son-John Hopkins s/o Levi, land formerly belonging
        to Juda Cannon
    Jessey Dashiell,Isaac Hopkins to care for plantation
        until John is of age
    to gr.son-Levi Hopkins s/o Levi
    to gr.daus-Parthena Nicholson,Mary Cooper, Eunice Cooper,
        Sarah Ellingsworth,Ann Ellingsworth
    to gr.son-Thomas Cooper and gr.son-John Samuels
    to dau-Mary Roberts
    wit;George Dashiell,Henry Dashiell,Jessee Dashiell,
        Joseph Dashiell

MAGRATH,John   16 Nov 1751   14 Jul 1752
    to wife-Mary, 1/3rds,lands
    to eldest son-David, pt.three trs. OWENS IMPROVEMENT,
        MIDDLE, OWENS DELIGHT (desc.) bounds plantation where
        Mary Fallis lives. tr. REFUGE
    to son-Levin (under age),bal. of lands
    to son-John, pt. of afsd trs.(desc.)on road from Princess
        Anne to Muny bridge. If no issue to son Levin
    wit;Owen Magrath,Jane Weatherly,Elizabeth Waggamen
        came Henry Waggemen made oath

                            f.14
HORSEY,Isaac of Coventry Parish 31 Jan 1752   11 Jul 1752
    to dau-Sarah Bozman, exec. dwelling plantation COULBOURN
        216a.(desc.)
    to dau-Sarah Bozman 250a. marsh PLAIN HARBOR
    to gr.daus-Betsy Layfield,Mary Laws after decease of my
        dau. Sarah and George Bozman.
    to gr.dau-Ann Schoolfield
    wit;Smith Horsey,Thomas Dixon,Ambrose Dixon

                            f.14
HARRIS,Caleb   8 Sep 1751   19 Aug 1752
    to son-James, 1 shilling
    to son-Abraham, land FLEMMONS LOSS 60a.
    wit;Jacob Williams,Mary Williams,John Tull

                            f.15
McGRATH,Jane   21 Oct 1751   8 Sep 1752
    to dau-Esther McGrah, dwelling plantation left me by
        my son Robert
    todau-Martha Phebus
    wit;Henry Ballard,David Macgrath,Jane Weatherly

                            f.15
ANDERSON,John   15 Feb 1752   20 Mar 1752
    to eldest son-James, house and lot in Princess Anne Town
        lying in back of lot formerly belonging to Patrick
        Allison whereon the Publick house always stood. (James
        to be apprenticed to a house carpenter or joiner at
        age 15)
    to wife-Rachel, exec.,guardian of two trs.BECKFORD, and
        ANDERSONS ADVENTURE
    140a. of ANDERSONS ADVENTURE that bounds Major John Elzey
        in or near Pr.Anne to be sold to John White of Princess
        Anne, merchant
    wit;John Geddis,John Done,Christopher Maughan
                            f.15-16
TOWNSEND,Benjamin   17 Nov 1751   19 Mar 1752
    to sons-John and Joshua
    to youngest son-Samuel, land I live TOWNSENDS SITUATION
        306a., if no issue to my youngest dau. Mary Townsend
    to gr.son-Benjamin Dashiell
    to wife-Mary, 1/3rds, exec.
    to children-Susannah and Samuel
    wit;Joseph Dashiell,John Walter,John Cox

VINCENT,Thomas   21 Dec 1738   22 Nov 1752
    to son-Thomas,estate
    wit;Purnell Johnson, Wm.Bready (died by probate)
    came Isaac Handy who wrote the will

f.16-17

COTTINGHAM,Charles   5 Feb 1753   22 Aug 1753
    to wife-Anne, ½ dwelling plantation
    to son-John,exec.,pt. tr.BOSTON, tr.GOSHEN
    to children-Charles,Thomas,John,Rachel, tr. my father
        Thomas Cottingham bou/o Stephen Horsey HORSEY DOWN
    to three sons-Marsh in Condockway marshes
    wit;Thomas Addams,William Addams,Samson Wheatly

f.17

KILLETT,Eunice   22 May 1753   23 Jul 1753
    to dau-Elizabeth Kellett
    to son-Robert, land bou/o Robert Ridgly, If he dies without
        issue to friend Henry Lowes
    to cousins--Sarah Henry, Mary lHandy d/o John, Ellinor
     Dashiell d/o Henry, ¡Priscilla Dashiell d/o Levin
    Henry Lowes exec.
    wit;Isaac Handy,Jane Gillis,Ann Irving

f.17-18

WRIGHT,Thomas   8 Feb 1753   27 Feb 1753
    to wife-Rebeccah,exec.,dwelling plantation.Afterdeath to
    son-Henry, he to make over all his right to land on Little
        Creek that was bou/from David Polk 200a to my son
        Gowan Wright and 100a to my son Thomas Wright by name
        of WHITTYES RIDGE. Tr. MUSKETTS HALL
    to gr.children-Ann Polk, Robert Polk
    to dau-Sarah Windsor
    to daus-Mary Wright, Harris Ballard
    wit;George Irving,Panther Laws, Thomas Martin

f.18

VINCENT,Thomas   7 Apr 1752   23 Mar 1753
    to wife-unnamed, exec. 1/3rds
    to son-Matthias,100acres
    to son-Isaac, Dwelling plantation, 100a.adjacent
    to sons-Jonathan and James
    to dau-Sarah
    wit;Benjamin Byrd,Major Dorman,George Green

f.18

READ,Mary widow of John   4 Feb 1753   20 Feb 1753
    to gr.dau-Mary Huggens
    to dau-Hannah Huggens
    to son-James Read,exec.
    to-son John Reads dau.Margaret, son Zachariah Reads dau.Anne,
     to son Obediah's dau. Sarah, son-James Reads daus. Mary
     and Susannah
    to son-Hezekiah
    wit;Solomon Truitt,Aaron Mezick,Covington Mezick

ELZEY,Sarah   21 Jul 1747   25 Mar 1753
    tosister-Elizabeth Elzey
    to nephews-Robert Elzey 2nd.son of bro.John, James Elzey
       s/o John
    to neices-Mary Stoughten d/o sister Ann Stoughten, Sarah
       Elzey dau/o bro. John
    to kinsman,Arnold Elzey
    to nephew-Arnold Elzey Jr.(exec) s/o brother John
    wit;John Elzey,Arnold Elzey,Robert King

f.19-20
ROBERSON,John   5 Nov 1748   19 Jul 1753
    to son-James, 150a. pt. tr.IRELANDS EYE
    to son-John, 100a s/s of Plumb Creek LONG DELAY
    to son-Jacob, 150a. and dwelling plantation
    to children-Ann Roberson and William Roberson
    to wife-Mary,exec.
    wit;Thomas Cooper Walter Derby,Mitchell Dashiell

f.20
DAVIS,Bridget   1 Feb 1754   14 Sep 1754
    to daus.-Abigail,Ailcee,Sarah,Bridget,Anne
    to sons-Arthur, William
    friends-Ralph Milbourn to apprentice son William, David
      McDonald and Samuel Handy to oversee estate
    wit;Richard Hall,John Waters

f.20-21
JOHNSON,Samuel   5 Aug 1750   22 Aug 1753
    to wife-Elizabeth, 1/3rds. exec.
    to son-Benjamin, land where I live willed me by my
      father FRIENDS CHOICE
    to dau-Mary Johnson, tr. COLD HARBOUR in Worc.Co. on
      Broad Creek
    to daus-Joanna and Sarah
    wit;Isaac Handy,Purnell Johnson,Sarah Johnson

f.21
JONES,Elizabeth   13 Jul 1749   21 Aug 1754
    to dau-Margaret Ballard, dau.Ellinor Leatherbury
    to son-William,sons-George,Thomas, Benjamin
    to gr.son-Robert Jones s/o John Jones (under age)
    to-son William Jones' son John, son Robert Jones' son John
    wit;Joseph Dashiell, Panther Laws

f.21-22
LEATHERBURY, John   29 Nov 1753   23 Apr 1754
    to son-Thomas, lands on Quantico
    to daus-Betty and Eleanor Leatherbury
    to wife-Eleanor,exec.
    to sons-John and Charles
    wit;Thomas Jones,Benjamin Jones,John Jones

f.22
DAVIS,William   8 Feb 1752   5 Mar 1754
    to son-in-law-Joseph Allen and dau.Betty Allen dwelling
      plantation(desc.) bounds John Williams line, 60a. adj.
      FORTUNE and 1/3 orchard. Joseph Allen exec.
    to wife-Bridget,exec.,Dwelling house, lands. after death to
    gr.son-William Davis Allen (under 21)

cont'd

DAVIS,William, cont'd
    to gr.son-John Allen
    to cousin-Davis Baley (under 16)
    wit;David Polk,Matthew Goslee, Joshua Turpin

f.22
JACKSON,Samuel   11 Feb 1753   9 Apr 1754
    to wife-Sarah,exec.,dwelling plantation
    to gr.son-Samuel Jackson Baley, exec., plantation JAXONS
      LOTT, if no heirs to
    gr.son-Beajamin Baley
    to gr.ch.-Betty,Steven,David,Jonathan,Sarah,George,Mary
      and Eleanor Baley
    wit;William Tully, Thomas Magee

f.22-23
WRITE,Betty   16 Feb 1754   5 Mar 1754
    to sister-Easter Right, the 1/3's my husbands estate
    to two sons-Zebulon and Steven Right
    wit;Thomas Phillips, Isaac Parremore,Thomas Dashiell

f.23-24
PHILLIPS,Richard   10 Oct 1754   31 Dec 1754
    to wife-Alse,exec.,plantation
    Thomas Holbrook, William Pullott to assist administration
    to sons-John, James(under 21)
    wit;William Giles,George Bennett,John Dawson

f.24
WATERS,Elizabeth Sr.   20 April 1752   20 Apr 1754
    to son-Richard, 91a.left me by Thomas Everton, pt. two
      tracts FLATT LANDS, JOHNSONS RIDGE between the Anna-
      messex River and Manokin
    to dau-Sarah Waters, bal. of 2 trs. afsd., exec.
    to son-Littleton Waters' youngest children, Elizabeth,
      Esther and Dolley (under age)
    to-gr.son-Richard Waters
    to-Esther Lowes, Elizabeth Waters d/o William, Elizabeth
      Hutchens
    wit;Ephraim Wilson,Henry Landen,Ann Dorman

f.25
MELSON,Samuel   25 Nov 1753   19 Feb 1753
    to brother-Benjamin ½ estate
    to sister-Ann Graham, ½ est. and then to her son Jehu
      Parremore(under age)
    Henry Graham,exec.
    wit;George Lewis Gastineau, Morgan Cordery,Bridget Cordery

f.25
DAVIS,Arthur   12 Nov 1740   4 Feb 1754
    to 3 eldest children-Mary, John, Richard
    to wife-Bridget
    wit;David Wood, David Mackmorie, Richard Hall

f.25-26
POLLETT,Priscilla   12 Nov 1753   19 Feb 1754
    to sister-Sarah Pollitt,bond passed from Christopher Dowdle
    to mother-Sarah Dowdle
    to brother-John and brother George Pollett
    wit;William Roach,Betty Roach,Stephen Roach

f.26-27

LINDOW,Rebeccah —   26 Dec 1753   25 Aug 1755
   to bro-in-law-Arnold Elzey, lands on Pocomoke River in
     Worc.Co., exec. (refers to him also as brother)
   to-Doctor Thomas Denwood and his wife Mary
   to son not-yet christened, to be named Thomas Dashiell
   to sisters-Margaret Elzey, Martha Rencher, Elizabeth
     Cemey and two children George Denwood had by my sister
     Mary Denwood
   wit;Henry Waggamen,Charles Leatherbury,James Trahearn

f.27

TURPIN,William   27 May 1755   8 Nov 1755
   to son-William
   to gr.daus-Sarah King,Elizabeth King,Elizabeth Turpin,
     Sarah Turpin
   to gr.sons and gr.daus. children of William McClemmy dec'd.
   to son-Whitty, land bou/o Barnaby Willis. exec.
   wit;William Fountain,Barnaby Willis,John Waters

f.28

MOOR,William   4 Apr 1759   20 Jun 1755
   to son-Thomas, 61a. s/s of tr. in Nanticoke,exec.
   to sons-Charles, Shiles,John, William,Risdon
   to wife-Elizabeth, 61a.afsd lands, then to son Charles
   to gr.daus-Elizabeth d/o Alexander Rickets, Elizabeth Winsor
   wit;Charles Rawlins,Joshua Edge,Nehemiah Edge

f.28-29

ADDAMS,George   2 Oct 1752   20 Dec 1755
   to dau-Rachel Addams, pt.of plantation on e/s Green Branch
   to son-Jacob Addams, orchard next ot my brother William
     Addams. Balance of afsd. land
   to daus-Jean Beauchamp, Sarah Lord (exec.)
   to gr.son-Henry Lord
   wit;Hope Addams,William Addams,Samuel Addams

f.29

JONES,William   17 Agu 1754   13 May 1755
   to son-Thomas,exec.,100a. in Manokin adj. Samuel Owens
   to son-John, all tract pur/o John Alexander between
     Wiccomico Creek and Manokin Town. Land adj. except
     100a. given son Thomas
   to gr.daus-Sarah Addams, Mary Addams
   to son-in-law-Peter Spencer Hack
   to wife-Mary,exec.
   wit;Robert Jones,Thomas Dashiell,Levin Dashiell

f.30

MITCHELL,Robert   7 Mar 1753   8 May 1755
   to son-Joshua,exec.,plantation where I live GOOD SUCESS
   to wife-Mary
   to son-Isaac, exec., tr. bou/o Joseph Lankford and Mary
     Smith 250a MIDDLESEX, WILLIAMS HOPE (if no issue to son
     Josiah
   to dau-Parthenia Heath widow of Dorman Heath
   wit;John Hamilton,William Williams,Sarah Hamilton

9

BALLARD,Henry   11 Jul 1755   29 Jul 1755
    to sons-Charles,Levin,Thomas
    to daus-Priscilla Mitchell w/o Stephen, Eleanor Ballard,
      Ann Ballard
    to wife-Mary, 1/3rds, exec. after death or marriage to
    son-Robert, exec. 2/3rds Real estate. He to discharge
      debt from me and my son Levin to Samuel Ritchie
    wit;Robert Jenkins Henry,Thomas Denwood,Mary Denwood

GOSLING,John   11 Jul 1755   2 Dec 1755
    to wife-Joanna,lands. after marriage or death to
    son-William-
    to children-Esther,Lear,Priscilla,Ann,William,Marah,
      Daniel and dau.Jean Jones
    wit;Jonathan Stott,Jane Stott,Daniel Scilly

KING,Robert, Esq.of Somerset Co. residing in Accocomac Co.Va.
             13 May 1753   26 Jun 1755
    to son-Nehemiah King,exec.
    to-Richard Waters s/o William dec'd by his wife Abigail,
    tr. of marsh LONDONS ADVISEMENT near head of Teague Creek
    to-William Walston and Thomas Walston, bal. of afsd marsh
      that lies n/ward of Waters Ditch and within what was
      formerly called Benjamin King's pasture
    Whereas Edward Waters pur/of me lands on Stevens Branch
      (desc.) title to be conveyed to him.
    to son-Nehemiah, dwelling plantation in Manokin where my
      father Major Robert King lived 300a. KINGSLAND. If no issue t
    gr.son-Thomas King of Robert, lands s/s of Gr.Annemessex River
      1566a.
    Whereas my son Robert King died leaving sons Thomas and
      Robert Jenkins King, I give to Robert J. TIMBER TRACT
      on Stevens branch bounds Aaron Tilman and Edward Cluff's.
      Lands in Worc. Co. owned by son Robert 200a to be sold.
    All 75a. Cypress Swamp pt. of tr. CONVENIENCY on Pocomoke
      River in Worc.Co. conveyed by deed from Peter Collier
      and others to my deceased sister Mary Hampton andmyself
      to sisters eldest son Robert Jenkins Henry
    to gr.dau-Mary Barnes(under 16) d/o Major Abraham
    to gr.dau-Mary King d/o Nehemiah
    to wife-Ann,exec.,estate on e/shore of Virginia. Money due
      from Moses Mills & Joseph Stevenson of Wor.Co. & from
      Alexander Buncle in Va. Lands bou/o John Lankford
    to nephews-Major Henry Ballard,Col.John Henry,Robert Jenkins
     Henry-
    to neices-Sarah Leatherbury w/o John, Elizabeth Dashiell w/o
      Charles
    to Reverend John Hamilton
    wit; Jarvis Ballard,Revell Horsey,John Givans,John Lecatt
    codicil 12 Jul 1754-to gr.son Robert Jenkins King pt. tr.
      WHARTONS FOLLY. wit;Levin Wilson,Joshua Riggin,Rachel
      Slokam
    codicil 27 Feb 1755. To wife Ann prop. at Virginia Plantation
      and at Tangier Islands. wit;William Burridge,Revel Horsey,
      Jonathan Shockley,William Horsey,John Macome

ADAMS,Collins   none   24 Mar 1755
   to wife-Tabitha, plantation where I live. exec.
   to son-Jacob, ½ tr.on road from Rehobeth to Ralph
     Milbourn's next to Isaac Dickeson(desc.) HOUSTONS CHOICE
   to son-Phillip, bal. of afsd lands. Pt. SNOW HILL (desc)
     tr. COLLINS ADVENTURE
   to eldest dau-Sarah and daus.Abigail,Tabitha, Anne Mary
   to son-Samuel Collins and son Isaac (under 21)
   wit;Samuel Collins,John Collins,Joshua Donoho,Samuel Collins Jr.

f.38

HANDY,Samuel   2 Nov 1754   1 Apr 1755
   to wife-Mary, 1/3rds. lands and houses. exec .
   to son-Samuel, Bal. of lands. tobe cared for by my brother
   in-law Littleton Dennis until age 21
   to daus-Mary and Elizabeth
   to son-John gun had of William Whitaker and to son William
   wit;Thomas Handy,John Dennis Jr.,Littleton Dennis

f.38-39

BROUGHTON,John   10 Jan 1755   22 Mar 1755
   to son-William, plantation where I live WILLIAMS HOPE 100a.
     and to his wife Jemima and then to his son John(under 18)
   to dau-Esther Broughton, and dau. Hannay Riggin
   to son-John Jr. exec. pt. land bou/o Thomas Linsey. Also pt.
     WILLIAMS HOPE (desc.) w/s Freemans Branch. 50a.HOG QUARTER
   wit;Cornelius Ward, Thomas Maddux,John Perkins

f.39

SCOTT,Robert   9 Jan 1753   22 Mar 1755
   to son-John, plantation where I live
   wit;Thomas Tull,Naomi Kilsick,William Fordred(dec'd by probate)

f.40

VINCENT,James of Stepney Parish 29 Nov 1754   9 Apr 1755
   to son-Joseph,dwelling plant. 75a. BATCHELLORS CHOICE. If
     no issue to son Benjamin
   to son-Jacob, balance of lands 50a.
   to wife-Sarah and all my children
   wi;Thomas Moor,William Moor,Shiles Moore

f.40

LANKFORD,Thomas   11 Mar 1752   25 Mar 1756
   to son-Thomas,exec.,dwelling plantation
   to daus-Mary Lankford,Ann Price
   to gr.son-Benjamin Lankford
   wit;Richard Green,Meshack Green, John Anderson
   came Widow Judea Lankford, demands 1/3rds

f.41

PARREMORE,Benjamin   27 Apr 1756   28 Sep 1756
   to son-Joseph, 50a. PARRAMORES MISFORTUNE, if no issue to
   brother-Joseph Parremore
   to wife-unnamed, 1/3rds exec.
   wit;John Williams,John Calloway,Mitchell Relph

f.41-42

HANDY,John, Capt.   5 Nov 1756   28 Dec 1756
   toson-Levin, lands on Wicomico River. If no issue to child
   my wife is now with to be called John.   cont'd

HANDY,John,-cont'd.
    to wife-Ann, 1/3rds.exec.
    to son-Thomas, plantation where I live (desc.) adj.William
       Nutters
    to unborn child, lands QUARTER PLANTATION
    to dau-Emelia Handy
    friends-John Henry and Ephraim King and brothers Samuel
       Handy to advise. execs.
    to son-Levin, he to live with his gr.mother(my mother)
    wit;Thomas Gillis,William Windsor,Sarah Handy,Mary Handy

                  f.42-43
LEATHERBURY,John   1 May 1756   17 Nov 1756
    to son-Charles,lands on Wicomico Creek purchased of Isaac
       Noble Sr. and Isaac Noble Jr.
    to gr.son-John Leatherbury
    to daus-Elenor Leatherbury, Sarah McClester, Mary Leatherbury
    to dau-Elizabeth, land SCHOOL HOUSE RIDGE
    to son-John,dwelling plant. in Gr.Money bou/o Margery and
       Phillip Covington
    to son-Robert, lands bou/o George Harris on Wicomicco River.
       Tract bou/o Thomas Covington COVINGTONS FOLLY. tr. MY
       -OWN BEFORE. exec.
    to-William Astin, pt. tr. on Quantico Branch being pt. of
       tr. the upper pt. sold to Richard Harris, conveyed me
       by Ahab Costen
    to wife-unnamed. plantation during widowhood. exec.
    wit;Charles Ballard,John Dorman,George Day Scott

                  f.43
HEARNE,William   11 Jun 1741   20 Jan 1756
    to son-Elijah Hearne, 175a. pt. STAINS, to include dwelling
       plantation where I live,exec.
    to son-Isaac, 150a. pt. afsd tr.
    friends-Benjamin Handy and George Hearn to divide prop.
    to son-Samuel,Jonathan,Benjamin
    to daus-Hannah, Mary Freeney,Sarah Tindal
    wit;Isaac Handy,Nehemiah Hearne,Joseph Scrogin

                  f.43-44
DASHIELL,Henry   7 Sep 1755   20 Jan 1756
    to wife-Jane
    to sons-Thomas, exec., Henry,Arthur
    to daus-Mary, Elenor, Lear
    wit;George Dashiell,Thomas Dashiell,Hugh Porter

                  f.44-45
DASHIELL,Thomas Sr.   17 Mar 1755   7 Feb 1756
    to son-Henry, 2 parcels land between Tipqueen and Tyaskin
       Creeks s/s Nanticoke River, one pt. left me by my father
       BECKNAM 700a. After his death to his son Thomas.
    to sons-Thomas,Henry,Levin 250a. marsh n/s Wicomicco River
       SHILES FOLLY
    to son-Levin,exec. land in Whitehaven twon on Wic.River being
       pt. sold to Samuel Worthington
    Tr. SOMERSETT whereon Money Church now stands to that parish
    to gr.son-Thomas Dashiell son of George
    to daus-Betty West, Sarah Irving, Jane Gillis and her children
                                  cont'd.

DASHIELL,Thomas Sr. cont'd
     to gr.daus-Ann Coulbourn, Priscilla Willin, Mary Handy
        d/o John and my dau.Ann, Betty Handy w/o Isaac Handy,
        Betty Smith, Mary Nicholson, Sarah Henry d/o Isaac
        Handy, Priscilla Jones d/o son Levin Dashiell, Sarah
        d/o son Charles Dashiell, Ann Irving d/o George Irving
     to son-Thomas and his son Josiah
     to sons-Levin and Charles
     wit;Robert Jones,Thomas Jones,Robert Downes

f.45

LISTER,Jean   29 Mar 1756   27 Apr 1756
     to dau-Abigail Long wife of David Long
     to gr.sons-Littleton,Josiah,David Long sons of Abigail
     to dau-Leah Furnace w/o William
     to gr.dau.Priscilla Furnace d/o Wm. and Leah
     to son-Jessy Lister, tr. where I live
     wit;Isaiah Tilghman,Stacey Mills,Robert Beauchamp

f.46

PURKINS,John, planter   10 Nov 1755   22 Apr 1756
     to son-John, plantation where I live except 30a. on w/s
        Aquonticial Branch
     to son-William, tr. bou/o Alexander Maddux(desc.)adj.
        Gideon Tilmans field. 30a. afsd.(under 16)
     to daus-Sarah and Mary
     to wife- Mary, plantation,exec.
     brother-Michael Purnkins
     wit;James Hayman,Jonathan Cluff,Teague Riggin

f.46-47

BENSTON,George,planter   29 Dec 1756   7 Apr 1756
     to son-John,plantation where I live 100a WOOLVER
     to sons-Matthias and William
     to dau-Betsey Miles
     wit;Arsbol Stitt,George Gullett,Mary Maddux

f.47

DASHIELL,Clement   10 Jun 1756   20 Jul 1756
     to daus-Mary,Sarah and Nancy
     to son-Josiah,plantation where I live pt. 2 trs. DASHIELLS
        LOTT, CHANCE 450a. given me by my father George by deed
        of gift dated 10 Jan 1742 (minor)
     to son-Clement (minor)
     to wife-Sarah, 1/3rds, exec.
     to brother-Louther Dashiell
     wit;Charles Leatherbury,Benjamin Colttman,William Gray,
        Isaac Dashiell

f.48

LONG,Samuel, planter   13 Jun 1756   11 Sep 1756
     to wife-Sarah,68a. WILSONS LOTT. after death to son William.exec.
     to daus-Jean,Mary,Sarah
     to son-William, exec.
     to son-Randolph, marsh LONGS CHANCE
     to son-Jeffrey, tr. LONGS LELIGHT
     to son-Samuel
     wit;Nehemiah Turpin,Stacey Miles,Jessee Lister

```
                              f.48
GIBBONS,Thomas               19 Aug 1756          16 Sep 1756
    to daus-Mary,Ann,Elizabeth
    to sons-Solomon,Robert, John (all under 21)
    to son-Thomas, all lands
    wit;Elijah Tilghman,William Gibbons,Margaret Tilghman

                              f.49
KING,Sarah        —          13 Aug 1754           7 Sep 1756
    to gr.sons-Robert King, Hast Dashiell,William Francis
        Dashiell, John Stuart, William Stuart, Daniel Wailes
    to gr.daus-Elizabeth Dashiell,Martha Dashiell,Sarah
        King-Mackomorie,Wlizabeth Wailes,Ann Stuart
    to dau-Rebecca Dashiell
    to-child Joseph Wailes s/o Daniel
    to-Ellinor Russell
    bal. to gr.ch. children of Wm.Dashiell now dec'd and
        Rebecca Dashiell now wife of George Dashiell
    gr.son-Daniel Wailes and Day Scott execs.
    wit;Sarah Quattermus,William Donoho

                              f.49
BARKLOTT,John                21 Feb 1753          10 Nov 1745
    to son-John
    to dau-Alce
    to wife-Ann,estate.after death to son Alworth(Alworth exec.)
    wit;John Wallace,Bloyce Harris,Joseph Dashiell

                              f.50
FARRINGTON,William           1 Nov 1756           17 Nov 1756
    to dau-Rachel Carmical 190a. WARRINGTON
    to dau-Leah Dorman 225a. WEATHERLYS RESERVE
    to son-George Farrington,exec.,146½a. the upper pt. of
        293a. held by names SLIPE, PASTRING. WEATHERLEYS PURCHASE
        where my dwelling house is
    to gr.dau-Jane Farrington d/o dec'd son Levin (under 16)
    to son-Robert, the lower half of land 146a.
    wit;John Weatherly,Joseph Weatherly,Elijah Weatherly

                              f.51-52
DISHEROON,Michael            20 Oct 1756          29 Nov 1756
    to wife-Mary, dwelling plantation where I live 58a. pt.
        ACQUIS CHOICE
    TO son-Constant, dwelling plant afsd after wife's death
    to children-John,Mary, Josephus, Bannister,Elenor, Ann
        Starling,Margaret Dickeson
    wit;William Disheroon,Thomas Todvine,Joshua Porter

                              f.52
LOW,Ralph                    25 Feb 1750/1        17 Mar 1756
    to son-John, lands where he lives (desc.)
    to son-George,exec.,bal. of lands, if no issue to
    son-Hudson and Robert
    to son-Ralph,exec.,dwelling plantation(if no heirs to Hudson.
    to wife- unnamed, 1/2 plantation
    to daus-Sarah Henry,Margaret Phillips, Disia? Rachel
    wit;Thomas Robards,Richard Phillips,Robert Twilley
```

JONES,John   23 Dec1756   11 Feb 1757
    to sons-Robert and James Macmurray Jones, lands
    to son-James M., tr. DOWNES CHOICE, 100a. adj.JONES CHANCE
    to daus-Ann and Sarah
    wit;William Nutter,Richard Stevens Bounds,Hezekiah Dorman
    came Margaret Jones,widow demands rights

DENWOOD,Levin   25 Feb 1757   27 Dec 1757
    to mother and father (unnamed)
    to brother-George Waters and bro.John Waters,execs.
    to brother-Spencer Waters tr. in Dorc.Co. n/w fork of
      the Nanticoke
    to Betty and John Denwood children of my wife
    wit;Edward Waters Jr.,Elizabeth Waters,Elizabeth Reading

MILBOURN,Ralph   25 Mar 1757   27 May1757
    to son-Lodowick, tr. PRINCES GROVE n/s Pocomoke River,
     DALES ADVENTURE, exec.
    to children of son Ralph,(all under 16)
    to son-Joshua- tr. where he lives in Accocomac Co.Va.
    to son-Nathan, tr. adj.James Broadwater in Accoc.Co.Va.
    to daus-Matthew, Hezieh, M ary
    to wife-Hannah, 1/3rds,exec.
    to children-William,Isaac andJacob
    wit;Charles Ballard,Ephraim Evans,William Stockley

CHRISTIOPHER,John   29 Jan 1749/50   18 Aug 1757
    to daus-Hannah Gordy,Mary Christopher
    to-Grace Morris,Sarah Parris
    to son-Clement, plantation where I live
    to wife-Hannah
    wit;Christopher Dowdle,Hirom Reddish, Thomas Crouch

EVANS,Thomas   5 Nov 1757   24 Dec 1757
    to wife-Rease,exec. land OWEN GLENDORE where James Baker
     lives(desc.)adj.Jaboz Pitt 90a., to be laid off by
     Teague Riggin and Elias White
    to sons-Ephraim, Nathaniel,bal. of lands
    to daus-Leah Evans, Elizabeth Brittingham
    to-Levin Powell, Teague Riggin,Ralph Corbin
    toson-William Evans
    wit;Elias White,Lodowick Milbourn,,Jacob Milbourn

GRAHAM,Robert   13 Nov 1755   28 Dec 1757
    to son-John, lands, exec.if of age. to live with his
     aunt Grissey Graham
    to dau-Mary, to be under care of Mrs. Elizabeth Jones
    to son-Phillip, to be under care of Capt.Waggamen
    wit;Joseph Dashiell,Daniel Wailes,George Dashiell

COLLINS,Samuel   5 Jun 1744   24 Dec 1757
    to wife-Rebeccah,1/3rds,lands, exec.,during widowhood,then to
    sons-Samuel and John (both under 21)
    to daus-Mary and Margaret
    wit;John Milborun,Caleb Milbourn,James Nairne

COLLIER,Robert,Planter   3 Feb 1756   16 Nov 1757
    to wife-Ann
    to son-Douty, exec.
    to son-Robert, tr.COLLINS ADVANTAGE
    to son-George, 45a. MOUNT HOPE
    to daus-Jane Dashiell,Margaret Dashiell,Nelly Winright
      and Sarah Outterbridge
    to gr.sons-Roger Hopkinss/o John and George Collier
      Hopkins,Robert Hopkins
    wit;Archibald Ritchie,Joshua Jackson,James Anderson

f.57

HENRY,John   9 Feb 1757   3 Mar 1757
    to wife-Frances, 1/3rds
    to son-John, exec. lands
    to gr.dau-Francis Wiley
    to sons-Robert and Hugh
    to dau-Martha Wiley
    wit;John Pitts,Hudson Low,George Dean,Frances Wiley

f.57

DASHIELL,Benjamin   1 Apr 1756   17 Aug 1757
    to mother-Bridget
    to brother(unnamed) and sister Mary Townsend's children
      Uncle Joseph Dashiell (desc.)
    wit;Joseph Dashiell,George Dashiell

f.58

SCOTT,Day,   14 Jun 1753   17 Aug 1757
    to son-Geoge Day Scott,plantation where I live GREEN HILL
      being pt. of tr. SUNKEN GROUND beg. at mouth of Hast
      or Jonsons Creek(desc.) bounds tr. conveyed me by
      Col. Gale. Plantation where my father lived LOW HOUSE,
      Plantation and LAST CHOICE to be sold to pay debt
      due Col.Ennals
    to-George Dashiell Sr. 50a. out of LAST CHOICE
    to-Betty Fortune, tr. where she lives 50a,she to pay bal.due.
    to-John Shiles Sr.,for debts due him
    to-Sophia Scott who lives with me
    friends-Robert Jenkins Henry,Isaac Handy Sr.,John Handy execs.
    wit;Francis Chaney, Benoi Wheeldoon

f.58

BEAUCHAMP,John   9 Sep 1756   21 May 1757
    to wife-Mary,exec.,use of plantation during widowhood, then to
    son-John
    to children-Edward,Priscilla,Betts, Nancy
    brother-Thomas Beauchamp,exec.
    wit;William Beauchamp,Sarah Curtis,Marcy Beauchamp

f.59

MAC CLESTER,Neal of StepneyParish 11 Nov 1751   5 Nov 1757
    to nephew-Samuel McClester s/o elder Bro.John, tr. OAK GROVE
      on s/s Nanticoke Riber near plant.where Richard Phillips
      lived in Worc.Co.Md., tr.HWITE CHAPPLE near Parron Creek
      and bounds Gabriel Cooper. Lot #10 in Green Hill town. exec.
    wit;Stephen Hopkins,Jr., Charles Brown,Izabella Hopkins

BYRD,Thomas Sr.   1 Jul 1752   16 Mar 1757
    to son-Elgat, 150a. JESEMAN, 50a. ELGATS LOTT
    to son-Thomas,manor plantation, 50a.ELGATS LOT, 50a.
       HACILAH as was given to Sarah Byrd by William Elgate
    to son-Benjamin,plantation on Quantico Br.150a.PARTNERS CHOICE
    to daus-Mary and Betty
    toson-Joshua
    to wife-Catheron, balance. exec.
    Brother Benjamin Byrd exec.
    wit;Moses Driskell,Thomas Humprhis, Benjamin Byrd

FINCH,John   11 Mar 1758   22 Mar 1758
    to wife-Margaret, R.E. during widowhood, then to
    sons-John (exec.) and James
    wit;William Brown,George Twilley,Isaac Giles

TULL,Thomas   30 Oct 1757   28 Oct 1758
    to wife-Rachel, exec. lands
    to sons-William,Thomas,Charles,Handy,Samuel,Levin
    to daus-Rode, Rachel
    wit;Samuel Tull,Joshua Hall,Sarah Hall

PURKINS,Michael   1 Apr 1757   18 Nov 1758
    to-Ann Gibbins
    to-William,Sarah,John, Mary children of John Purkins
    to-Michael Purkins s/o Thomas
    to-Sarah Purnkins d/o William
    to-Thomas Purkins son of William
    to brother-William Purkins
    to-Michael Cluff (exec.),Jonathan Cluff, Patrick McLally,
       Abigail Harris
    wit;John Broughton,Alexander Maddux

CALLAWAY,William Sr.   20 Jan 1758   23 Mar 1758
    to son-Moses, 50a. WHAT YOU PLEASE,50a.Pt. IRON HILL(desc.)
    to son-Matthew, balance of IRON HILL, exec.
    to dau-Elizabeth
    to gr.children-Levin,Elisha,Mary,William,Joshua Hearn
    to wife-Elizabeth
    wit;John Williams,Moses Carmean,Joshua Waller

BLURE,Margaret   17 Sep 1746   8 Sep 1758
    to bro-in-law-John Killam
    to father,-Joseph MacClestor, exec.
    to son-Joseph Blure(under 21)
    wit;John Walter,George Dashiell Jr.,Neal McClestor(died by1758)

LAW,James   18 Aug 1757   21 Jun 1758
    to son-William, dwelling plantation THE ADDITION
    to son-James, tr. 100a DOGWOOD RIDGE
    to wife-Phillis, 1/3rds,exec.
    to son-John
    to daus.-Margaret Hobbs,Esther Law,Sarah Law
    wit;Henry Newman,Isaac Newman,Martha Newman,Wm.Brown Sr.

f.63

ADAMS,Tabitha   25 Apr 1758   2 Dec 1758
    to son-Phillip, plantation husband Collins Adams bou/o
        Moses Mills
    to sons-Jacob(exec.) and Phillip,land formerly belonging
        to Samuel Clogg
    to daus-Sarah,Abigail, Ann Mary
    tosons-Isaac and Samuel Collins Adams
    to brother-Samuel Adams
    wit;John Collins,Elias White

f.63

CALDWELL,Joshua   23 Jan 1758   4 Apr 1758
    to-Thomas Savdog??, 3 trs. BOLEY BEGIN,MAIDEN HEAD,
        CALDWELLS PERCHES
    tr.surveyed by Robert Caldwell ANYTHING to be sold
    to 5 sons (under 18), Eldest son William, to daus.(unnamed)
    William Venables,Joseph Scroggin to advise.
    wit;Benjamin Byrd,Joshua Venables,Nehemiah Hitch

f.64

WILLSON,John   19 May 1752   22 Mar 1758
    to youngest son-James, 1/2 tr. DERBIE near Barron Creek(desc)
    to son-David, other 1/2 tr.afsd. exec.
    to dau-Anne Robertson, tr.RATT BAND 145a.
    to cousin-Mary Wilson Taylor, 100a pt.WILSONS LOTT left
        her in my fathers will
    to son-Thomas
    wit;William Brown,Sarah Brown,James Brown

f.64

EVANS,John   20 Nov 1752   6 Mar 1758
    to wife-Arrabella,exec.,lands during widowhood, then to
    son-John,plantation where I live 200a.
    to son-Nathan, 100a.NORTH END, after death to
    Gr-son-Thomas Evans (under 21)
    to-Solomon Evans,Richard Evans,Tabitha Parks,Comfort
        Mister,Leah Evans,Rachel Evans,Ann Crockett
    Thomas Tylor,exec.
    wit;Solomon Bird,Thomas Tylor,David Bird

f.65

BOZMAN,Bridget   21 Apr 1759   22 Nov 1759
    to neices-Eleanor Bluitt(exec.),Rbecca Covington
    to nephew-Phillip Covington
    to sister-Eleanor Covington
    wit;Henry Lowes,Ann Stuart

f.65

DASHIELL,Benjamin   18 Apr 1757   4 Sep 1759
    to cousin-John Bunkol (under 21)
    to brother-Joseph Dashiell,exec.
    wit;Charles Ballard,Ellenor Stevens,Martha Bluitt(alias Dashei.

f.65-66

PIPER,Eleanor   3 May 1758   1 Jun 1759
    to mother-Rachel Caldwell,exec.
    to brothers-Christopher Piper,Matthew Piper
    wit;Christopher Piper,Sarah Nutter

HARRIS,Robert,planter   28 Sep 1755   13 Mar 1759
   to son-John,planation where I live, 315a. CHANCE, tr.
     PARTURAGE 50a.
   to wife-Abigail, 1/3rds,dwelling plantation
   to son-Zachariah, tr. HEATHS QUARTER 101a.,LITTLE WORTH
     50a.,LIBERTY
   to son-in-law-Samuel Acworth for his dau.Sarah's part
   to daus-Hannah Gray,Betty Listor,Abigail Harris
   wit;John Sheldon,William Fleming,Jane Fleming,Sarah Smulling

EDGE,Joshua   14 Jun 1758   21 Mar 1759
   to wife-Elizabeth,lands during widowhood,then to
   son-Nemiah,plantation,exec.
   to son-Joshua and dau.Abigail
   wit;Isaac Jones,William Jones,John Stilly

CALLOWAY,Moses   10 Nov 1758   21 Mar 1759
   to son-Moses, 25a. WHAT YOU PLEASE with plantation where
     John Calloway lived. pt. tr. IRON HILL
   to son-Clammond,25a. WHAT YOU PLEASE, plantation where
     William Calloway Jr. lived. pt. IRON HILL
   to son-Aaron(under 21)
   to wife-Ann,exec.
   wit;Matthew Calloway,Zekell Jones,Joseph Scroggin

STEVENS,William   30 Oct 1758   25 Mar 1759
   to son-John, plantation where I live and the Ferry,exec.
   to son-William, 100a.in Worc.Co. pt. COWLY, plantation
     50a.COLE
   to son-Ephraim, 150a. pt.PAYNES POINT
   to daus-Mary and Betty Stevnes
   to wife-Mary,exec.
   wit;Thomas Lambden,Jessy Brittingham,Moses Mills

BEAUCHAMP,Thomas,planter   28 Mar 1759   22 May 1759
   to wife-Betty, 1/2 lands, exec.
   to sons-Handy, Levin, lands where I live (desc.)
   to son-Thomas,bal. of lands
   to brother-William,lands (desc.) BEAUCHAMP ADVENTURE
   to-Fountain Beauchamp, Beauchamp Davis, lands(desc.)
   to daus-Naomey and Grace
   wit;Richard Boston,Beauchamp Davis Jr.,Mary Boston

ACWORTH,Thomas Sr.   3 May 1759   20 Jun 1759
   to son-James,Manor plantation, pt. tr. HOG QUARTER. pt.
     tr. ACWORTHS DELIGHT, exec.
   to wife-unnamed, 1/3rds
   to-son-Richard,exec.,plantation where he lives.Pts.afsd.(desc)
   to-William Acworth,upper plantation on Gastineau's line
     on road to Rewastico (son)
   to sons-Charles and Train, tr. ADDITION
   to 5 sons-100a.marsh MARSH POINT, 50a. RIDGES
   to dau-Temperance Acworth
   wit;Thomas Right,Sarah Young,George Lewis Gastineau

HANDY,Samuel   25 Dec 1758   24 Apr 1759
   to wife-Sarah, 1/3rds
   to son-John,balance, if no issue to
   nephew-John Handy s/o Charles in Rhode Island,if no issue to
   nephew-Levin Handy s/o brother John
   to nephew-Levin,to be in care of my mother Jane Gillis
   wit;Isaac Handy,William Winder,Henry Lowes Jr.

f.70
LANGCAKE,Francis   2 Mar 1754   23 Jun 1759
   to gr.son-Francis Langcake s/o George dec'd dwelling plant.
   to gr.son-William Langcake s/o Stephen,plantation where
     his father lives 150a.
   to gr.sons-Cannon Langcake s/o Stephen, Obadiah Disheroon
    s/o John,Francis Disheroon s/o John, Thomas Langcake
   to son-Stephen
   to-William Benston s/o William all lands in Worc.Co.
    near Gumb Branch and Broad Creek
   to gr.daus-Judah Benston,Magdalene Benston d/o William
   to son-in-law-William Benston and dau.Isabelle Benston
   to gr.dau-Judah Clarkson d/o James
   to-Rachel Woodgate, to live on my plantation in Worc.Co.
   to dau-in-law-Fran Clarkson d/o James
   wit;Joshua Humphris,John Elzey Jr.John Finch
   came-Rachel Lancake, claims lawful estate

f.71
HEARN,Nehemiah –   4 Mar 1760   7 Apr 1760
   to eldest son-Elisha,tr. STANES 125a.,dwelling plantation,
    tr. FEARFIELDS 37a.,exec.
   to son-William, tr.PLEASANT GROVE 50a. in Worc.Co.
   to son-Thomas, tr. SANDY HILL 75a.
   to son-Joshua,tr. FOLLY 30a. in Worc.Co.
   to wife-Bette, 1/3rds,exec.
   to dau-Mary
   wit;Joseph Scroggin,Elijah Hearn,Isaac Moore

f.71
SUMMARS,John-   13 Aug 1758   1 Nov 1760
   to eldest son-David, tr.(desc.)
   to daus-Mary Ward,Betty Summers
   to sons-Benjamin,Lazarus,Isaac, Richard
   to gr.son-Isaac Summers(under 16)
   to dau-Deborah Starling
   to gr.dau-Grace Starling
   to wife-Joanna
   wit;Jonathan Martin,Cornelius Ward, George Summers

f.71-72
BOZMAN,George   5 Mar 1753   20 Aug 1760
   to daus-Sarah Airs,Ann Schoolfield,Betty Layfield,Mary Laws
   to wife-Sarah, bal. of est. during widowhood. exec. then to
   son-George, exec.
   wit;Thomas Dixon,Ambrose Dixon,William Fordred(dec'd by probat

ADDAMS,William   21 Apr 1756   8 Dec 1760
    to son-William,exec. 2 trs. WHITLY,ADAMS CONCLUSION
       (desc.)on road from Coventry Parish to Stevens Ferry
    to son-Phillip-pt of ADVENTURE, pt.ADAMS CONCLUSION
       and afsd WHITELY (desc.)
    to son-Dennis, balance of lands
    to wife-Margrate
    to daus-Elizabeth Adams,Leah Schoolfield, Margrate
    wit;Samuel Adams,Sarah Adams,Catherine Adams,Ann Adams

f.73
HOBBS,Stephen   2 Nov 1760   12 Dec 1760
    to brother-Benjamin Hobbs,exec.,tr.HOBBS ADVENTURE. He
       to pay bond due Thomas Jones of Manokin
    to son-Josiah (under 21) to learn trade of sadler
    wit;Phillip Covington,Robert Austen,Henry Waggaman

f.73
WILLIAMS,John Sr.   29 Nov 1760   27 Dec 1760
    to eldest son-John,lands on e/s Turley Branch 200a.
       WILLIAMS LOTT, tr. 12½a.bou/o Edmond Beauchamp FIRST
       CHOICE, 20a. THE CONCLUSION, If he has no issue to
    son-Josiah, tr. MIDDLE STRAND 85a.
    to daus-Mary Polk, Hannah Harmanson,Priscilla Williams
    to sons-Jacob,Samuel,Benjamin
    to wife-Elizabeth, 1/3rds, exec.
    wit;Stephen Garland,James Curtis,Levin Williams

f.74
FARRINGTON,Robert   12 Nov 1759   10 Jan1760
    to wife-unnamed, exec., 25a. being Matthew Dormans pasture
    to sister-Rachel Carmichael's two sons, William, John
    wit;Roger Train,Joshua Whittington,Nelly Dowdle

f.74
DOUGHERTY,John   12 Feb 1752   5 Jan 1760
    to wife-Rachel,lands where I live, 1/3rds
    to son-Obed, land(desc.)bounds John Ward where Henry
       Lord lived. LITTLE USK, MEADOW
    to son-James, bal.afsd, pt. marsh LITTLE PASTOR(desc)
    to daus-Sarah,Jemima,Rachel,Martha,Grace
    to son-Nathaniel,Stephen,Peter,John,Ezekiel,Isaac
    sons-Isaac and Peter execs.
    wit;William Riggin,John Riggin,Rachel Riggen

f.75
PARKS,Arthur, Sr.   30 Aug 1743   9 Feb 1760
    to youngest son-Job,manor and tr.HOG NECK on Smith Island
       75a. being pt. tr. on Dogwood Ridge Creek. 150a.
    wit;John Evans,Thomas Tylor,Thomas Evans,John Evans Jr.
       Solomon Evans

f.75
MARSHALL,Thomas of Northampton Co. Virginia
                        19 Jan 1760   10 Mar 1761
    to two sons-Esme & Thomas John Marshall,execs.,lands in
       Naswodox Neck in this Co.(desc.) 100a. each adj.Holloway
       Bunting and John Brickhouse and Matthew Harmanson's dec'd.
       and 500a. bou/o Abner Brickhouse on seaside BRICKHOUSE
       MARSH
    to wife-Patience
    to daus-Patience Allen w/o William of Somerset Co.Md.
    to gr.son-Hezekiah Tilney(under age)
    wit;George Dashiell,Rose Fisher,Margaret Dusmuir

```
                          f.75
MEARS,John               1 Nov 1759          19 Mar 1761
    to sons-Robert,Ezekiel
    to daus-Mary Mitchell,Sarah Bartlett,Grace Surman,Betty Mears
    to wife-Dorothy,exec. plantation during widowhood, then
        to dau.Nelly Mealy
    wit;George Balley,Louther Dashiell,Clement Christopher

                          f.76-77
MEZICK,Jacob             22 Dec 1751          9 Feb 1761
    to wife-Elizabeth, 1/3rds, dwelling plantation
    to son-Jacob, Igave him all my lands except 17a.of lower
        pt. tr. JAMES LOT which I give to gr.son James Mezick
        s/o Elihu
    to children-Elihu,Joshua,Aaron,Covington,Jacob,Dinah
        Nelson, Rachel Ellengsworth
    wit;Thomas Mitchell,Morgan Landers,Jane Larramer (dec'dby
                                                      probate)

                          f.77-78
MILES,Henry              19 Nov 1756          4 Feb 1761
    to son-William,exec.,land HEARTS EASE, tr. HOG PEN SWAMP,
        75a. adj. DIXONS HAMMOCK
    to son-Henry,exec., entailed land, trs. WHITE OAK,SECURITY,
        FATHERS CARE, HOVEWELL
    to gr.son-William s/o Samuel and Rebeccah, tr. HAZARD,
        pt. of NEGLECT, 4a.
    to grson-Samuel s/o William, son Henry's land if no issue
    Son Henry to pay Alice Wheatly five pounds
    to daus-Mary Revel Bedsworth(widow) and her son Henry
        Bedsworth(under 13)and her son William Bedsworth
    to daus-Rebecca Miles and her dau.Rebeccah, Wineford Miles,
        Alice Wheatley
    to gr.dau-Rachel More
    to-Ann Frazer
    wit;John Haw,Daniel Cullin,Revel Horsey

                          f.78
CLUFF,Edward             3 Sep 1760          3 Jan 1761
    to son-Michael,exec.,manor plantation where I live, ½ Cypress
        Swamp, ½ tr. TIMBER GROVE
    to son-Jonathan, other ½ afsd lands
    to daus-Sarah Merrill and gr.dau.Sarah Merrill
    to-Scarborough Merrill
    to-Rachel Wait
    wit;John Peden,William Broughton,Neble Dreadon

                          f.78
MATTHEWS,Teague          23 Nov 1760          31 Jan 1761
    to gr.son-Benjamin Holland Matthews, 100a WORTHLESS (he
        is son of Phillip dec'd.) ½ marsh on w/s Morumsco Creek
        HAPHAZZARD, if no issue to
    son-David, Balance of lands and Marsh. exec. he to care
        for plantation until Benjamin is of age.  If David has
        no issue lands to
    daus-Tabitha, Betty,Sarah,Rebecca
    to wife-Elizabeth
    wit;Teague Riggin,John Matthews,John Riggin Jr.,Samuel Adams
```

f.79-80

WOOD,William   26 Oct 1760   25 Jul 1761
    to son-Levi,dwelling plantation,tr. DUBLIN,if no issue to
    son-William
    to son-Elijah
    to daus-Leah,Sarah and Martha
    wit;Purnell Outten,James Dakes,Elias Taylor

f.80

WARD,Samuel   7 Jan 1761   6 Jun 1761
    to son-John,exec.,land COWDAME RUN
    to son-Joseph,lands north of John's(desc.)
    to dau.-Kiziah Taws,lands(desc.), WHITE OAK SWAMP
    to dau-Martha Daugherty, lands (desc.)
    to son-Samuel, lands
    to dau-Mary Parremore
    wo wife-Mary
    Isaac Dougherty,exec.
    wit;William Riggin,Mathias Ward,Peter Lord

f.81-82

HORSEY,Stephen   8 Oct 1754   9 Sep 1761
    to wife-unnamed- dwelling plantation
    to gr.daus-Mary Elizabeth Fassitt, Mary Horsey
    to son-Revell, dwelling plant after wife decease. exec.
    to son-Stephen, lands between William Outterbridges and
       tr. HANNAH DELIGHT
    to gr.son-John Horsey (under 21)land out of WATKINS
       POINT (desc.)
    to afsd sons and gr.son-three trs. TONEYS VINEYARD in
       Wicomicco Creek. DESART between Annamessex and Manokin
       Rivers, lands belonging to Ann Tost north of patent
       EXCHANGE
    to Friend, George McClester lands on Tipqueen on Nanticoke
       River called WETPQUEEN with sons Stephen and Revel, divided
       equally, they to give Robert Colleir a small moiety of
       said lands where he lives
    to-Elizabeth w/o son John Horsey dec'd,plantation she lives
    to nephew-William Wheatly
    wit;William Miles,Stephen Moor, Henry Miles,James Hearn
    codicil 11 Jan 1759- to gr.son Isaac,lands on w/s creek
       between John Davis and my plantation except 150a. out
       of the patent called OLD UNDUE. 45a. out of COW QUARTER
       which 195a. my father Stephen Horsey sold and conveyed
       to Thomas Davis
    to friend-Jonathan Darkus, 50a. withing bounds of WATKINS
       POINT where he lives
    wit;James Gunby,William Miles,Aaron Starling

f.82-83

ACWORTH,Samuel of Stepney Parish 10 Jun 1761 11 Dec 1761
    to dau-Esther Acworth,exec.
    to son-Ephraim,lands on n/s Rowastico Creek, PINEYS ISLAND
       ADDITION TO ACWORTHS PURCHASE 375..
    to gr.daus-Sarah Bounds, Mary Watkins(under16)
    to wife-Patience,exec.
    wit;Day Givans,Matthew Dorman,George Farrington
    came-George Darrington age 23 yrs.made oath that Samuel
       Acworth died about the 13th of June. Came Matthew Dorman
       age 31 years says that John Watkins the testators son-in-
       law came.

WHITE,Stevens   27 May 1760   6 May 1761
     to wife-Betty
     to brother-Elias White,exec.,500a pt. lands I live, pt.
        REHOBETH, pt. CALDICUT (desc.)
     to son-William Stevens White (under age). Col.Robert
        Jenkins Henry to be his guardian
     wit;Robert Taylor,David Boston,Solomon Boston

SMITH,Henry of Coventry Parish 28 Jan 1746/7 31 Oct 1761
     to son-William,exec.,land out of tr.BALD RIDGE, pt. of
        Plantation where I live being pt. land deed of 8 Dec 1742
     to son-Henry,bal.afsd tr. Bond from William (son)dated
        10 Dec 1742 for lSMITHS LOTT. If no issue to
     dau-Sarah Lankford
     to gr.son-Archibald Smith
     son-in-law-Puzey Lankford,exec.
     wit;Benjamin Lankford,Robert Cargley(dec'd by probate)
        William Fordred(dec'd by probate)

KING,Whittington   1 Sep 1761   3 Nov 1761
     to son-Robert
     to son-John, tr. CHANCE, exec.
     Cousin-Jessee King trustee
     wit;Thomas Jones,Jessee King,John Parker

WEATHERLY,James   15 Sep 1761   6 Oct 1761
     to sons-James,Charles,Jessee,lands asfollows-son James
        Plantation where I live(desc.) adj.Cedar Landing. Son
        Charles,plantation where Joseph Tully lives adj.afsd.
        Son Jessee,lands beginning at upper Wadding Place on
        Rewastico Creek. Tr. WEATHERLEYS LOTT
     to daus-Ellenor,Sarah
     to son-in-law-Charles Hopkins
     to-Daniel Rodes,survey on Nanticoke River
     Friend-Joseph Weatherly, exec., he to see to school of
        my son James. Beauchamp Hull to bring up my son Charles.
     wit;John Weatherly,Joseph Husk,Joshua Parramore,William Nutter

WARD,Jacob   18 Dec 1760   2 May 1761
     to wife-Mary,dwelling plantation during widowhood, then to
     son-Stephen
     to sons-Isaac,Benajmin,Joseph (all under 21)
     to daus-Jemima,Mary and Betty
     wit;William Miles,William Juett,Jonathan Summers

WATERS,John   27 Mar 1760   28 Apr 1761
     to wife-M ary Elizabeth,plantation where I live, during
        widowhood, then to son John (exec.)
     to 5 youngest ch.--George,William,Edward,Littleton,Peter
     to son-Spencer
     to son-George Nicholas Sevein Waters,exec.,tr. HOGG YARD
        in Dorcester Co. n/w fork of the Nanticoke River
     to-John Teague of Worc.Co., tr. in Worc.Co. where he lives
     to-John Denwood s/o Levin
     to-Esabel Selby w/o Ezekiel, she to give son Spencer release
        of rights to land pur/o Levin Denwood in Dorcester Co.
     to five youngest sons, land on Potatoe Neck
     wit;Henry Lowes,William Waters Jr. George Waters Jr.

f.87

LOWES,Tubman   31 Dec 1758   28 April 1765
    to friend-Edward Waters to settle business in common
        with him from 1 Jan. 1759
    to-Aunt Sarah Waters
    to-Elizabeth Waters of Philadelphia
    to-Ellenor Stevens for keeping my house and family
    to cousins-Elizabeth Waters(Marine),Esther Waters,Dolly
        Waters,Elizabeth Windsor,Francis Windsor,John? Hogdon,
        Elizabeth Hollis and Frame
    Bond of Dr.Andrew Francis Cheney to each of my godsons
        of said Andrew
    to father and mother-Henry and Esther Lowes(Henry exec.)
    to brother-Henry Lowes
    to-Sarah Waters,Ann Waters,Ebn.Stevens
    Edward Waters Jr.,exec.
    Frinds-William Allen,William Hayward,James Dickenson,
        James Allen,John Gibson of Philadelphia
    wit;Joseph Dashiell,Matthew Waliss,Littleton Waters

f.88-90

WAGGAMEN,Henry   18 Sep 1759   25 Jun 1761
    to wife-Mary,1/3rds,lands, exec.
    to son-John,land on Gr.Money tr.WAGGAMANS PURCHASE, pt.2
        trs. ABBINGTON,CARNEYS CHANCE, lands on Broad Creek
        which spewoth out of the Manokin River
    to sons-William Elliott Waggaman, Henry and George
    to son-John Elliott Waggamen to be kept at school by Rev.
        Mr. Finley until age 18
    to son-William Elliott,(under 21) tr.on s/s Manokin River
        WAGGAMONS LOTT. He to be in care of Levin Gale
    to son-Henry,lands on s/s Wicomico River CALCUTTA, pt.2
        tr.s VULCAN VINEYARD,NICHOLSONS LOTT pur/o Charles
        Nicholson (under 21)
    to daus-Sarah,Elizabeth,Mary (all under 16)
    Friend.Levin Gale, exec.
    wit;Mary Brown,William Hayward,Henry Jackson,John Jennor
    codicil-to son George ½ pt. lot in Princess Anne Town
        pur/o Nehemiah Dorman. That half where house that Thomas
        Bond lives. The other ½ to son William Elliott.18 Sep 1759
    codicil-daughter Mary Waggaman now dec'd -11 Dec 1760
    wit;Ralph Pomeroy, Ephraim Wilson

f.90

GIBBINS,Amey(widow)   9 Nov 1762   15 Dec 1762
    to brother-William Perkins
    to-John, Sarah,William Perkins ch. of John dec'd
    to-Thomas and John Gibbons s/s of my dec'd husband
    to cousins of Sarah Perkins dec'd my wearing apparel
    to cousin Mary Perkins d/o dec'd brother John
    Friend-Michael Cluff,exec.
    wit;Betty Wheatly,Sampson Wheatly

f.90

KILLAM,Edward   12 Jan 1757   16 Feb 1762
    to gr.son-Edward Kellam,dwell.plantation,lands on n/s Barren
        Creek except 50a.sold to Stephen Rose, 100a.sold to Matthew
        Gaskenew where they now live. plantation KELLAMS DISCOVERY
    to son-John Kellam,exec.,to keep son Edward until age 21
    to gr.daus-Isbal Kellam,Margaret Kellam,Sarah Kellam
    wit;John Brown,Robert Brown, George Brown

```
WHITE,John          6 Feb 1761          7 Jan 1762
    to wife-Elizabeth, 1/3rds, dwelling plantation, then to
    to son-John, Balance of FRIENDS CONTENTMENT, OXFORD 100a.
    to son-William,exec.,108a. pt. of tr.FATHERS AND SONS DESIRE
        tr. FRIENDS CONTENTMENT
    to eldest daughter-Ann Jones
    to daus-Margaret Neal wife of John
    wit;JohnLaws Jr.,Francis White,John Windsor
```

f.91
```
MUNRO,Alexander          26 Feb 1762          18 Mar 1762
    to youngest sons-Isaac and Matthias
    friend-William Pullett,exec.
    wit;John Tull,Sinah Harris
```

f.91
```
DISHAROON,William          25 Jan 1762          23 Feb 1762
    to wife-Mary,exec.,dwelling plantation, 150a. FRISOLLS
        ENJOYMENT, during widowhood,then to
    to son-Levin,exec., afsd plant.& tr. 50a.COME NO NEIGHER,
        if he has no issue to son James
    to daus-Margaret,Eunice,Priscilla
    to sons-Jessee,Weatman,Joshua,James
    wit;John Watson,John Disheroon,John Carrow
```

f.92
```
ADDAMS,David,planter          7 Dec 1761          20 Feb 1762
    to wife-Mary,exec.
    to children-Betty Addams,Martha Lankford,Mary Owen,Sarah
        Addams, Isaac Addams, Rhoday Addams,LeviAddams, Mary
        Addams,Nanney Addams, Ann Adams, William Addams, David
        Addams(exec.)
    wit;Purnell Outten,Thomas Potter,Henry Potter
```

f.93
```
RAWLE,Joseph          23 Jul 1761          16 Feb 1762
    to-Matthew Karvin of Dorc.Co.,tr. in Dorc.Co. MONOCOY
        near Hungar River
    to-John Rotton of Dorc.Co.,tr TIMBER YARD
    to brother-Benajmin Rawls,exec.,and sister Jean England
        of Philadelphia
    to three ch. of cousin Francis Rawles dec'd of Philadelphia
    wit;Joseph Cope,David Cope,William Kennerly
```

f.93
```
HITCH.Solomon          24 Oct 1761          18 Nov 1761
    to wife-Elizabeth,plantation and land until son is age 18
    to son-Risdon
    to dau-Susannah
    wit;George Vinson,John Hitch Jr.,Thomas Humphris Sr.
```

f.93
```
HEARN,Thomas          27 Jan 1762          26 Mar 1762
    to sons-George,Ebenezer,Thomas (exec.)
    to daus-Elizabeth w/o Isaac Moore,Jemima Hearn,Sarah Hearn
        and Ann Hearn
    to gr.sons-Elisha Hearn,William Hearn and Joshua s/o Nehemiah
    to son-John,100a. HEARNS VENTURE, 50a.ST KITTS, tr. TOWER
        HILL 50a.
    to daus-Mary w/o Joshua Morgan,Esther w/o Benjamin Vincent
    to-James Hearn s/o William,150a. STAINS out of tr. of 420a.
        near Coxes Branch
    wit;John William,s,Elijah Hearn, George Martin
```

HOFINGTON,Thomas   20 Apr 1759   17 Aug 1762
    to son-Thomas,dwelling plantation BAKERS FOLLE
    to daus-Sarah Day, plantation HUFFINGTONS LOT
    to wife-Margaret
    to daus-Easter and Betty
    to eldest son-Richard
    wit;William Brown,George Brown,John Brown

f.94-95

WALSTON,Joy   2 Apr 1762   31 Jul 1762
    to cousins-Joy Walston,Jessee Walston,John Walston,Deba
      Roach,Ebey McDaniel,Rebecca Walston
    to brothers-Boaz and William Walston
    wit;Peter Hammond,William Hammond

f.95-96

DAVIS,John of Coventry Parish 25 Mar 1762   10 Aug 1762
    to nephew-Thomas Handy,exec, dwelling plant, Lower pt.
      land(desc.) taken up this 1st.day in the presence of
      Jacob Cullin, Thomas Montgomery,Stephen Dye where one
      Kelly now has his landing place on Johnsons Creek
      (desc.of lands) 34a. adj. Lazarus Lankford. Pt. LONG RIDGE
    to nephew-Samuel Cox,exec. upper pt.,where he lives (desc.)
      Tr. DAVIS INLET. 50a. Pocomoke Bayside near Johnsons Creek
    to eldest son of John Cox dec'd(whose name I do not know)
      100a. ANGLOSEY adj. to where his father William Cox
      lived and where my sister Mary Cox now lives
    to neices-Sarah Fleming w/o John, Elizabeth Coulbourn w/o
      William, Mary Goute formerly widow of one Randol of Kent
      Co. Md.
    to-Emilin Salsbury
    wit;Thomas Montgovery,William Roach,Stephen Dyes
    Codicil 23 Jul 1762-wit;includes Jacob Cullin

f.96-97

NELSON,William   4 Apr 1762   31 Aug 1762
    to gr.son-William Atkinson,70a. where I live. pt. NOBLE
      QUARTER bou/o John Evans dec'd. 25a. bou/o Edward Willin
      EDWARDS LOTT, 50a. bou/o John Evans Jr. pt. of NOBLE
      QUARTER, 25a.b/o Thomas Dashiell. (under 18)
    to wife-Ann
    to son-in-law-Isaac Atkinson,land at Muddy Hole where he lives
    to gr.sons-Joshua Atkinson,William Atkinson
    to dau-Betty Atkinson
    wit;Nicholas Evans,George Collier,Joseph Dashiell
    codicil dated 24 May 1762- wit;includes Jacob Mezick Jr.

f.97

LONG,Jeffrey   18 May 1762   17 Jul 1762
    to daus-Orpha Brittingham,Mary Long,Asseneth, Easter Long
    to son-Saywell, lands (under 21)
    to dau-Orpha, land below Coulbourn Long's
    to wife-Sarah,exec.
    wit;Hope Addams,George Miles,William Turpin

PHILLIPS, John   13 Aug 1762   25 Oct 1762
    to gr.son-Nathaniel Smulling, 50a. WOLF PITT RIDGE
    to son-John,exec.,balance of land. If no heir to
    daus-Elizabeth and Grace Phillips
    to son-in-law-William Layfield
    to wife-Elizabeth
    wit;Cornelius Ward,William Sullivan,Matthew Ward

WALLACE,Matthew   19 Jul 1761   25 May 1762
    to wife-Mary,exec.,dwelling plant. Land in Rock Creek
    to son-Joseph, afsd lands. If no heirs to
    son-David
    to sons-William,Richard, James
    to daus-Bridget Reavill,Mary Roe,Elizabeth Travis, Leah
      Wallace,Mary Wallace
    to-Ann Windsor d/o my wife Mary
    wit;George Jones,Gowan Wright,William White

BUTLER,Nathaniel   24 Apr 1760   16 Jun 1762
    to wife-Elizabeth, exec., and to her heirs. lands,estate.
    wit;Stephen Harris,Samuel Phebus,William Ballard

COOPER,Samuel   10 Dec 1760   25 May 1762
    towife-Priscilla, 1/3rds, dwelling plantation.
    to son-Samuel,plantation BEDFORD. exec.
    to dau-Ann Cooper
    to son-Leving
    wit;John Finch,William Gravenor,Thomas Gravenor

COSTEN,Ahab   2 Oct 1756   17 Jun 1762
    to wife-Abigail
    to sons-Ahab and Oliver
    to-Benjamin Cottman, 100a COSTONS VINEYARD where he lives
    wit;Isaac Costin,Joseph Thomson,Ambrus Fitzwaters

HITCH,John   9 Sep 1762   16 Mar 1763
    to son-Joshua,plantation where he lives. 150a., exec.
    to son-George-Plantation where he lives
    to children-John,James,Joseph, Baty Rencher
    to dau-Sarah Talbard and son-in-law John Talbard
    to wife-Baty
    wit;Joshua Humphris,Nathan Colver,Stephen Ellis

DARBY,Walter   4 Jun 1762   7 Mar 1763
    to wife-Sarah,lands BACHELORS CHANCE,DARBEYS ADDITION
    to sons-Thomas and William, afsd.lands after wife's death,
      DARBEYS ADVENTURE. If no issue to
    sons-Daniel,John,Benjamin
    to daus-Mary More,Margaret Rider,Elizabeth Wright
    wit;Isaac Taylor,James Taylor,Jacob Wright

COLLIER,Ann,widow   26 Dec 1761   10 Jan 1763
    to sons-Dowty,Robert, George
    to daus-Jane Dasheill,Sarah Outterbridge
    to gr.sons-George Collier Hopkins,John Hopkins,Robert
      Hopkins,Roger Hopkins sons of John Hopkins Sr.
    to dau-in-law-Priscilla Collier
    to four daughters(unnamed)
    wit;Archibald Ritchie,James Anderson

REVILL,Charles   1 Oct 1757 at Yorktown Va.-7Jan 1763
    to friends-William Miles, Revill Horsey,lands
    wit;Thomas Archer of Yorktown Ca.,William Stevenson,
      Edmund Tabb, Major Samson Wheatly

HANDY,Isaac   7 Dec 1760   24 Feb 1763
    to son-Thomas,land pur/o Rebeccah Bready alias Evans.
      Land bou/o Spence in North Carolina. If no issue to
    son-Isaac
    to son-William, 270a. pt. PEMBERTON (desc.)adj.land I
      bou/o Purnall Johnson and Mulberry Landing. If no issue
      to my son Isaac
    to son-Henry, Balance of PEMBERTON. SURVEYORS MISTAKE
      deeded me by my son George. (under 21)
    to son-George and all sons, marsh Cedar Hammocks on
      the Wicomicco River
    to cousin-Isaac Handy, tr. at Muddy Hole where he lives
    to-Thomas Willin Sr.,225a. of Marsh he bou/o me.
    to dau-Ann Handy
    to son-Isaac, money due me in Mr.Bacons and Mr. Beels
      hands in England.
    to wife-Ann, 1/2 plantation
    Gurdians, the Rev. Hugh Henry, Rev.John Harris, Robert
      Jenkins Henry, Capt.Henry lows, over sons Isaac,George
      and Thomas
    wit;Joshua Porter,Josiah Dashiell,Sarah Bartley

MADDUX,Thomas   19 Nov 1762   23 Feb 1763
    towife-Elizabeth
    to son-John, exec.
    to dau.-Ann Hall wife of Zorobable Hall
    to gr.son-John Tull
    to gr.son-Thomas Hall s/o Joshua
    wit;Lazarus Maddux,Lazarus Maddux Jr.,Edward Waters Jr.

ADDAMS,David of Worc.Co.   26 Sep 1763   4 Nov 1763
    to sister-Sarah Addams, Nanney Addams(exec.)
    to-William Addams and Mary Owens
    wit;John Dolbe,Thomas Hansle

ADDAMS,Samuel   1 Jun 1763   5 Jul 1763
    to-Caleb Boulden, tract originally in Somerset Co.but now
      in Worc.Co. on Broad Creek, TURKEY TRAP.

cont'd.

ADDAMS, Samuel, cont'd.
    to-son Samuel, exec., lands bou/o Jonathan Tull. Pt. of
      land bou/o Stephen Costen and John Harper (desc.)
    to son-Phillip Collins Addams, bal. of lands on s/w side
      Dividing Creek(desc.) under 21.
    to-Both sons tr. on w/s Morumsco Creek HAPHAZZARD
    to daus-Sarah Addams, Mary, Betty, Catherine, Ann Addams
    to wife-Sarah, plantation where I live in Morumsco
    wit; Samuel Matthews, William Addams Jr., Elias White

WINRIGHT, Stephen   1 Jan 1763   9 Feb 1763
    to son-Stephen(under age)
    tobro-in-laws-John Evans and Nicholas Evans to care for son
    to son-Cannon, 82a. that is 50a. of WITTONEYS CONTRIVANCE
      and 30a. out of IGNOBLE QUARTER bou/o Charles Dashiell
    to dau-Sarah Thorns
    to wife-Mary
    to 6 children-Evans, Ellender, John, Cannon, Stephen, Rebecca
    wit; Joseph Dashiell, John Evans, William Winright

HENRY, Hugh   8 Nov 1762   16 Mar 1763
    to wife-Sarah
    to son-Isaac, lands. To be under care of his gr.father Isaac
      Handy, Gent.
    to sons-Hugh and James (both under 21)
    to son-William Blair lHenry
    to brother-James Henry, guardian to Wm.B. and James
    to daughter-Nancy Henry
    wit; Thomas Handy, William Handy, Hannah Evans

COULBOURN, William, planter 17 Nov 1761   23 Oct 1764
    to wife-Jean, exec.
    to sons-William, Samuel, Solomon, Michael, Elijah(exec.), Stephen
    to dau-Mary Ellegood
    to gr.dau-Elizabeth Eskridge
    wit; William Miles, Nehemiah Hearn, Charity Watts

DEAN, Charles   23 Mar 1764   11 Sep 1764
    to son-Ephraim, 100a out of tract. If no issue to
    son-Abraham
    to son-Charles, dwelling plant. 100a.Adj. If no issue to
    son-Noble
    to-son-James, land on upper side of Walters Rode
    to-John Badley, 5a. where his house stands
    to son-Levie, 70a.
    to wife-Sarah
    wit; Levin Lingo, John Huffington, William Badley

POWELL, Levin   18 Jul 1760   23 Agu 1764
    to wife-Rachel, exec., plantation where I live. Marsh on
      Morumsco Creek COW QUARTER
    to son-Levi, afsd plantation after wife's death
    to son-Levin, marsh COW QUARTER
    to dau-Leah Maddux
    wit; Henry Schoolfield, Isaac Bozman Schoolfield, Wm.Schoolfield

```
                          f.108
JONES,Daniel            25 Apr 1758         27 Jul 1764
    to wife-Elizabeth, 1/2 dwelling plantation
    to son-Daniel, 1/2 dwelling plantation
    to son-Phillip, tr. COX CHOICE, 100a in Sweetwood bou/o
      Nehemiah Covington and Phillip Covington. 20a. bou/o
      James Covington
    to-Elener Covington
    toson-James
    to dau-Elizabeth Jones
    wit;Charles Dashiell,Charles_Leatherbury,Phillip Covington
                          f.108-109
WALLIS,Richard          20 Jan 1763         19 Jul 1764
    to--wife-Easter
    to-Hudson Low,100a. he pur/o me on s/s of CALDWELLS LOTT
    wit;Robert Jones,Mary Price,Dolly Mackluer
                          f.109
BURGIN,William          15 Feb 1764         20 Mar 1764
    to dau-Sarah
    to wife-Mary
    wit;Charles Woolford,Isaac Newman,Thomas Newman
                          f.109
JACKSON,Joshua          14 Feb 1764         2 Apr 1764
    to daus-Rachel Donoho,Surfiah Jackson
    to brother-Samuel Jackson
    to sons-John,George,Elihu,William
    to wife-Sarah,exec.
    wit;William Ellingsworth,James Beard
                          f.109
WILSON,Abigail          1 Aug 1764          23 Oct 1764
    to son-Richard Waters
    to daus-Elizabeth Waters,Sarah McClemmy w/o Whitty
    to son-James Wilson,exec.
    wit;Joseph Gillis,Sarah Waters,Levin Wilson
                          f.110
BENSON,Mary  --         7 Dec 1761          4 Oct 1764
    to gr.dau-Nancy Nicholson,land where my son John Nicholson
      lived. -
    to gr.dau-Mary Nicholason,land where I live on s/s of Weslow
      Neck. To be in care of my sons-in-law Doubty and Robert
      Collier until Mary is age 14.
    to dau-Priscilla Collier
    to dau-in-law-Mary Nicholson
    to gr.children-Nancy,Mary,Priscilla and Peggy Nicholson,
      Mary Bownes, Bridget Collier,Elizabeth Collier,Leah
      Collier,Luezar Collier, Milla Jackson,Mary Jackson,
      Betts Collier,Doubty Collier Jr., Nehemiah Crockett.
    to gr.dau-Alse Jacksons heirs, Ann Crockett,Levin Crockett,
      Elizabeth, John, Bridget Crockett
    to gr.daus-Mary and Priscilla daus/o John Nicholson
    to gr.dau-Bridget Crockett
    to-John Nicholsons,Joseph Nicholsons, Bridget Colliers childr
    wit;George Irving,Thomas Irving,Sarah Irving
```

```
                        f.110-111
WARD,Joseph               9 Mar 1765          28 May 1765
    to son-Cornelius, tract where he lives
    to daus-Mary Conway,Sarah Adkins
    to gr.son-Joseph Conoway s/o Levin and Mary
    to son-Jsoeph,plantation where I live
    to sons-Stevan and James(exec.)
    to gr.daus-Mary Shores,Aliss Shores
    wit;William Warwick,John Tull,Martha Warwick

                        f.111
WEATHERLY,Joseph          19 Mar 1764          12 Aug 1765
    to son-John, lands (desc.)
    to son-Joshua,lands at mouth of Barren Creek and marsh
       on the Nanticoke River    (all sons under 18)
    to son-Constantine,lands(desc.), ½ Cherry Tree Island
    to dau-Lotura Weatherly
    to wife-Patience
    to cousin-John Weatherly,lands(desc.)PARTNERSHIP
    to James,Charles and Jesse Weatherly, tr. ADDITION that I
       conveyed to their father James Weatherly since being
       resurveyed and now called PARTNERSHIP
    to-Charles Weatherly, 2a. pt. of WEATHERLYS POND
    friends-William Turpin and John Kellum,execs.
    wit;Mary Weatherly,George Farrington,Joseph Hurst

                        f.112
GODDARD,John              28 Sep 1760          28 Oct 1765
    to son-Francis Lane Goddard,pt. tr. DAYS BEGINNING
       ½ of 290a. on Broad Creek(desc.)
    to son-George, other-half afsd land
    to youngest daughter-Sarah
    to gr.son-John Goddard
    to wife-Sarah,exec.
    wit;William Robinson,John Robertson,John Williams

                        f.112-113
PAREMORE,Isaac            31 Mar 1765          29 Apr 1765
    to son-James,tr. where I live 50a PURCHASE (under 21)
    to son-Thomas (under 15)
    to wife-Abigail,exec.
    wit;Joshua Paremore,Henry Acworth,William Davis

                        f.113
HICKMAN,William of Stepney Parish 23 Feb 1765  1 Jul 1765
    to son-William, tr. NEW CASCEL
    to daus-Catheron Hickman alias White, Elizabeth Hickman
       alias Seairs
    to sons-Jonathan,Richard,William,Arthur
    wit;Samuel McClestor,Hugh Porter,Maccl.Porter,William Walter

                        f.113-114
COTTMAN,Ebenezer          9 Nov 1760          19 Mar 1765
    to dau-Phillis,exec.,dwelling plantation SAINT GILES 100a.
       Land on w/s road from Quantico Mill to Spring Hill Chapel
    to gr.son-Nathan Cottman s/o dau.Sarah Lowe, land WEATHERLEES
       ADVENTURE 200a.
    to daus-Mary Moor, Ann Waller
    son-in-law-George Low,exec.
    wit;Richard Green,Ralph Lowe,Hudson Lowe
```

COULBOURN,William,planter 4 Feb 1765   21 Mar 1765
    to wife-Elizabeth,exec.,2 trs. POMFRET,Fathers INTENT
    to son-John, afsd lands after wife's death
    to sons-Isaac,William,Thomas
    to sons-John and William,marsh on Joans Island 37a.
    to daus-Mary, Rachel
    to brother-Isaac Coulbourn and cousin Elijah Coulbourn guardi&
    wit;William Miles,Isaac Coulbourn,Elizabeth Coulbourn

DICKESON,Teague of Stepney Parish 15 Feb 1764 21 Jan 1765
    to wife-Ruth
    to dau-Leah Daugherty
    to son-Levi Dickeson,land on Broad Creek PASTORE
    to gr.son-Isaac s/o Levy Dickeson
    wit;Robert Walter,William Walter,John Graham

DASHIELL,Louther   26 Nov 1764   3 Apr 1765
    to daus-Jean, Milcah
    to son-Louther,dwelling plant. CHANCE(desc.), DASHIELLS LOTT
    to son-Arthur,pt. dwell.plantation(desc.)bounds land given
      by Col.George Dahsiell to Louther Dashiell
    to son-William, tr. bou/o Isaac Dashiell, pt. DASHIELLS LOTT
    to son-Matthias, pt. CHANCE
    to wife-Ann,exec.
    to brother-Thomas Dashiell
    wit;Thomas Dashiell,Isaac Dashiell,George Dashiell

MAGEE,Peter   16 Dec 1762   20 Aug 1766
    to son-John,exec.,75a. RICH RIDGE bou/o Thomas Gillis
    to daus-Magdalene Magee,Jane Collins
    to son-Thomas
    wit;John Williams,James English,James Jones

HOPKINS,John   14 Jan 1755   28 Jun 1766
    to wife-Elener
    to son-George Collier Hopkins,land at Cagors Strats
    to sons-John,Robert,Collier,Roger
    to son-John, tr. JOHN CHANCE in Worc.Co.,50a.adj. bou/o
      William Bensten
    to dau-Elizabeth Hopkins
    wit;Aaron Mezick,Benjamin Dashiell,Jessee Dashiell

CULVER,John-of Stepney Parish 2 Sep 1755   20 Apr 1766
    to sons-John,George,Thomas,Charles
    to sons-Moses and Aaron,land and dwelling plantation
    wit;John Taylor,Willia Taylor,Robert Twilley
    came, Mary Culver widow,demands 1/3rds

FULLERTON,Alexander   31 Mar 1766   25 Jun 1766
    to son-James,lower end of plantation
    John Watkins to have his 50a.
    to son-Tubman, balance of plantation
    to dau-Leah
    to son-Charles and wife Mary, exec.
    wit;Joshua Turpin,John Redish,Nicholas Redish

MARTIN,Thomas   14 May 1760   27 May 1766
    to wife-Isbal, 1/3rds. exec.
    to sons-Robert,Thomas,William,James,Henry
    to daus-Peggy, Nelly,Marry
    to son-John, dwelling plantation
    wit;Gowan Wright,Thomas Aickman,David MacDaniel

f.118
SHILES,Elizabeth   25 Mar 1765   24 Jun 1766
    to-John Crockett and his sister Elizabeth (my god-daughter)
    to-William Winrights wife Elizabeth (my god-daughter)
    to godson-Thomas Willin
    to-Elizabeth Ballard d/o Charles
    to-Ann Fleulling, Eliza McKintier and Wm.Venables 1st.daughter
    wit; Joseph Dashiell,William Willin

f.118
LANKFORD,John Sr.,painter   3 Jun 1766   18 Jul 1766
    to dau-Esther, ½dwelling plantation. She to pay for Elijah
      Lankfords schooling
    to gr.son-Edward Langford, other ½ plantation
    to-Rachel Collins d/o Edmund and Eleanor Collins
    to sons-John and Thomas(exec.)
    to daus-Ann Gupton w/o John and Esther Langford
    wit;John Anderson,George Law,Ralph Lowe

f.118
WINRIGHT,Stephen   4 Jul 1766   7 Aug 1766
    to wife-Elenor,plantation in Worc.Co. ADDITION TO GRUBB HILL
    to son-Zadock, afsd.plant. after wife's death. If no issue to
    youngest brothers-Solomon(exec.), Levin and John
    wit;Thomas Dasheill,George Collier Hopkins,Solomon Winright

f.119
COOPER,Thomas   4 Feb 1766   20 Aug 1766
    to eldest son-Abraham,plantation and ½ lands
    to son-Thomas,other ½ lands
    to wife-Isbel, 1/3rds
    to my four children,(unnamed.)
    wit;David Cordry,Samuel Cooper,William Tully

f.119
HUGGINS,Benjamin   21 Nov 1765   24 Jul 1766
    to wife-Ann and her three children(unnamed),exec.
    wit;John Span Conway,William Rencher

f.119-121
HENRY,Robert Jenkins,Esq.   21 Jul 1764   14 Nov 1766
    to wife-Gertrude, lands 1/3rds. exec.
    to son-Robert Jenkins Henry(now about 9 years old) 2/3rds
      lands. Manor Plantation where I live called MARYS LOT
      400a. being pt. tract Rehobeth. Tr. HENRYS ADDITION 50a.
      138½a. pur/o Sayward Tomlinson being pt. MANLOVES LOT.
      1/3rd of LIMBRICK being pt.of SONS CHOICE. Tr.GLASGOW 72a.
      all adj.to each other. Tr.WHITLEY RECTIFIED adj.neighbor
      James Dikes 245a. Pt. HIGNETS CHOICE and all lands at mouth
      of Morumsco Creek where James Smith mulatto lives. Tr.LONG
      MEADOW where John Long is now overseer 646a. Lands in Worc.
      Co. at Cypress Neck. Also after my wife's death her portion.
cont'd

HENRY,Robert Jenkins Esq.cont'd
    to son-Robert Jenkins-land on Pocomoke River devised me
      my the will of Col.Robert King, pur/by him and my dec'd
      mother Madam Mary Hampton
    to son-Edward, tr. FAIR MEADOW RECTIFIED where Benjamin
      Henderson the younger is overseer 535a. Tr.PET SHORE left
      me by my mother on Hornkill Creek in Sussex Co.Del. on
      Deleware Bay. Tr. HOROROTSON 640a on Merottuck River in
      Chowan Precinct North Carolina pt. of land pur/by my
      dec'd father John Henry of Co.Mosely.(under 21)if he dies to
    daus-Mary King Henry,Ann Henry,Elizabeth and Gertrude Henry
    to dau-Mary King Henry,tr. GOLDEN LYON on Morumsco Creek
      pur/o Charles Riggin 278a. 20a. marsh adj.pt. LONG MEADOW
    to dau-Ann Henry,tr. PROVIDENCE at Dividing Creek 400a.
    to dau-Elizabeth tr.FRIENDS ASSISTANCE near plant. where old
      Mr.John Caldwell dec'd lived 300a. If no issue to dau.Gertrude
    to-friend James Sherod of Terryl Co.in North Carolina for
      bond dated 25 Mar 1763 and when he pays up bond I give
      him land HUNUNTOK per contract.
    Whereas Mr.William Allen of Worc.Co. agreed to give me tr.
      SECURITY in Worc.Co. adj.Solomon Townsends, 51a. in pt.
      satisfaction of a debt due me from Francis Porter; if he
      pays for said to have title. otherwise exec. to sell land
    The land whereon the Presbyterian meeting house in Rehobeth
      not stands to the people of the congregation of Pocomoke
    The parcel whereon the Parish Church of Coventry stands to
      the people of the parish.
    The parcel whereon the Inspection House at Rehobeth stands
      to the publick use.
    Friends, Isaac Morris, Levin Gale and brother John Henry to
      settle the accounts of the Brig Friendship and company
    To-Martha Hall, a young woman who has lived in my family.
    to Brother-John Henry and Dorothy his wife. Brother Lloyd
      and cousin Betsy Lloyd
    Brother John Henry and Littleton Dennis to settle affair about
      the Cypress Swamp I agreed with Robert Nelson, that is ¼pt
      of tr. NEWFOUNDLAND in Worc.Co. If Mr.Dagworthys claim be
      settled, I devise the ¼ pt. pur/o Nelson to son Edward
    The negros given me by the Honorable ColEdward Lloyd to daus.
    Brother Lloyd, brother Henry and kinsman Nehemiah King and
      friends Levin Gale,William Hayward,Samuel Wilson Esq. to
      council wife and children
    Brothers Honorable Edward Lloyd of Talbout Co.Esq. and Col.
      John Henry of Dorcester Co. guardians
    wit;William Schoolfield,George Schoolfield,Henry Schoolfield
      John Jordan,Matthew Hopkins Jr.

FURNACE,James   4 Dec 1765   13 Jan 1767
    to son-William,exec.,dwelling plantati on where I live
    to son-George, two tr.sSOMETHING WORTH, WOLFS DEN(under 21)
    to sons-Jonathan(under 21) and James(exec.)
    to daus-Sarah, Judith Furnace, Elizabeth Cordray
    to wife-Sarah
    wit;Isaiah Tilghman,Jessee King,Aaron Tilghman

SHEPARD,William,Mariner of Whitehaven
                    14 Sep 1765   9 Nov 1766
    to wife-Alice, two houses in Whitehaven on Brackon Street
      and wages due on board Ship Sally, Capt.Charles Courtney
      commander
    wit;Charles Courtney,William Wilson,John Elzey Jr.

                    f.123
DASHIELL,Jeane   24 Dec 1765   8 Aug 1766
    to gr.dau-Jean Collier d/o Nicholas Evans Collier, exec.
    to gr.son-Roger Nicholas s/o Roger
    to brother-Doubty Collier
    to gr.ch.-Betty, Nichols,Henry,John,Thomas and Isaac
      children of my son Roger Nichols
    to gr.ch-George, Nicholas,Priscilla Collier ch. of Nicholas
      Evans Collier
    Brother-Doubty Collier and Isaac Hopkins to assist exec.
    wit;Aaron Mezick,George Dashiell

                    f.123
ALLEN,Joseph   1 Jan 1766   15 Jul 1766
    to son-William Davis Allen,lands
    to dau-Mary Lockerman Allen, negro girl in possession of
      Isaac Cooper that was devised by my father-in-law William
      Davis to my son John now dec'd.
    to wife-Betty,exec.
    wit;David Polk,William Allen,Thomas Dashie ll

                    f.123-124
COVINGTON,Jessee   10 Jun 1759   11 Mar 1767
    to brother-Abraham Covington
    wit;Charles Leatherbury,Phillip Covington,Daniel Jones Jr.

                    f.124
FLEWELLING,Samuel   11 Jun 1766   16 Feb 1767
    to son-Richard,plantation where I live 25a. or ½ tr.
      CLEAR OF CANNON SHOTT
    to son-John, tr. PRICKELLS COCKS HOTT andADDITION to same.,
      tr. COW RIDGE
    to son-Samuel,land bou/o John Beard. 25a. bal.CLEAR OF CANNON
      SHOTT
    to daus-Ann, Mary and Rebecca
    wit;Jacob Aires,Joseph Dashiell,Littleton Airs

                    f.124
LEONARD,Joseph   none   5 May 1767
    to son-Joseph,exec.,plantation 40a. PLUMPTON SALT ASH,
      50a. adj.LEVENS CHANCE, 50a. COXES ADVICE, 20a.CORDWINDERS
      HALL
    to son-John, 75a. pt. COXES FORK, 65a. HOLDERS BHANCE. Bond o
      Ebenezer Handy to John Trahearn assigned to me
    to wife-Jane 1/3rds
    to son-Michael Leonard's(dec.d) three children, Benajmin,
      Betty and Nelly (all under age)
    to dau-Ellener Gordy
    wit;Joseph Scroggin,William Twilley,Priscilla Crouch

DORMAN,David   14 Jan 1767   29 Apr 1767
>to wife-unnamed, 1/3rds
>to dau-Leah(under 16) in care of friend James Phillips
>daus-Betty and Sarah in care of brother Matthew Dorman
>to sons-David(under 14) in care of brother Matthew Dorman
>friend-John Crockett, to sell ands pur/o Hezekiah Read. exec.
>wit;Ephraim King,James Phillips,Zachariah Read

f.125-126

TILGHMAN,Joseph,planter   29 Sep 1763   27 Apr 1767
>to eldest son,Isiah, exec.,two tr.sBEANS HALL 100a.,
>   AMITY 196a.
>to dau-Margaret wife of James Hayman
>to daus-Elizabeth,Mary, Sarah Tilghman
>to son-Joseph,Manor plantation THOMSONS ADVENTURE 50a.,
>   JOSEPH FOLLY 66a.(under 21) if no issue to
>son-William, two tr.s MATTHEWS RIDGE 60a., SAPLINS RIDGE
>   19a. ADDITION TO SAPLINS RIDGE (under 21)
>wit;James Furniss,Alexander Porter,Levin Wilson

f.126

WRIGHT,Zebulon   9 Jan 1767   2 Feb 1767
>to wife-Alice,land. After death to my seven sons(unnamed)
>wit;Isaac Cooper,Joseph Cope,John Cooper

f.126

LAYFIELD,Robert   26 Oct 1766   27 Jan 1767
>to sons-Solomon,John, Jessee, George
>to wife-Rebeccah,dwelling plantation where I live
>wit;John Chambers,James Roach,George Disharoon

f.126

DORMAN,Hezekiah of Stepney Parish 22 Oct 1766 8 Jan 1767
>to daus-Elizabeth and Ann,dwelling plant. MORRISS'S LOTT
>to wife-Mary,exec.
>to daus-Elenor,Sarah Dorman,Prissy Jones
>to gr.dau-Mary Jones
>wit;George Walter,James Willin,Stephen Rowe,John Piper

f.127

KING,Nehemiah   29 Dec 1766   10 Jan 1767
>to wife-Frances,1/3 dwell.plantation. Plantation bou/o
>   Spencer Hack. after death to
>son-Robert, exec.,lands FOXENS, land bou/o Spencer Hack
> and Wm.Thompson, 1/3rds that belonged to the widow of John
> Horsey. Marsh on Devils Island
>to son-Nehemiah,(under 21),lands on Kings Branch between
>   Isaac Mitchell & Zorabable King &Piney Island & Little
>   Devils Island
>to son-Levin (under 21) plantation on Back Creek bou/o the West
>   between lands of Irving and Bannester Mitchel .Parcel
>   bou/o John Seon on Wicomico River. Land between Annemessix
>   River and Manokin River
>to dau-Mary King,land from my mother near Parkers Mill. Parcel
>   between Broad Creek and Nanticoke conveyed me by James West
>Friends-Rev.Mr.Kerr, Levin and Samuel Wilson to attend to
>   the education of my sons Nehemiah and Levin
>friends-John Henry,Levin Gale,Jacob Ker,Levin Wilson,Revill
>   Horsey to advise children
>wit;William Strawbridge,Jenkins King,Samuel Carter

JUET,William,planter   19 Oct 1765   18 Mar 1767
     to son-Nathaniel,exec.,dwelling plant. if no issue to
     gr.son-William Juet son of John
     to daus-Martha Juet,Betty Miles,Leah Juet,Roda Leek,
       Mary Juet, Cateron Juet
     to son-William, plantation at head of Nanticoke River in
       Dorcester Co.
     to wife-Mary, exec.
     wit;Purnell Outten,Elijah Conner,Bell Maddux
     came-JohnJuett, heir at law._did not object to will

                         f.128-129
LOWES,Henry   26 Jun1761   24 Jul 1767
     to wife-Esther, 1/3rds
     to son-Tubman,exec.(now missing)If he returns, dwelling
       Plantation pur/o heirs of Levin Gale Esq. PRIZE HOUSE
       or LOWES POINT. House and lot in Princess Anne town.
       Land mortgaged to me by March Fountain. 1/3rds bal.
     to son-Henry,exec., bal. 1/3rds
     Hewett Nutter conveyed title to lands on Wicomico River
       now in possession of Mr.Alexander Robinson, I give to
       said Hewett Nutter.
     to-Richard Biglands(he to pay his sister Mattux) land
       made to me by Joseph Calloway
     to neice-Ann Waters,plantation at Broad Creek pur/o Henry
       Windsor
     House on Chappel Street in Whitehaven to be in trust with
       Mr.Thomas Hartley and Sons, and Mr.John Gale until sold
       and ¼ pt. to my sister Mehitabel Hodgeson, 3/4pt to
     sister Elizabeth Hughes and her heirs. To my neices
     Elizabeth and Frances Windsor and Elizabeth Hollis.
     to-Eleanor Stevens,Ann Stewart,Elizabeth Stewart, James
       Stewart.
     Whereas a patent granted me in 1743 called LOWES ENLARGED
       that bounds LITTLE BELLAINE and includes the now plant.
       of Robert Killott, I give to said Robert.
     to the Charity School in Talbot County
     wit;Edward Waters Jr.,Margaret Lucas,Peter Derrix

                         f.129-130
ADAMS,Sarah   11 Mar 1767   9 Jun 1767
     to dau-Cathron Harper
     to daus-Mary,Ann,Betty Adams
     to sons-Phillip Collins Adams, Samuel Adams(exec.)
     to gr.dau-Sarah Harper
     wit;Purnell Outten,Boaz Matthews,Sarah Matthews
                         f.130
GRAHAM,John   6 Feb 1767   11 Jun1767
     to aunt-Grissy Grame
     to brother-Phillip,lands (under 21)
     Friend-Daniel Wailes,George Day Scott,execs.
     wit;Robert Collier,Betts Collier

```
                            f.130
TURPIN,William          15 May 1767          19 Aug 1767
     to wife-unnamed, 1/3rds
     to son-Joshua, tr. bou/o Nathaniel Dougherty 100a.(under 21)
        100a. SAMPIER being pt. of ADVENTURE. If no issue to
     son-William
     to son-John,exec.,land where I live. Plantation bou/o
        Benjamin Cottman
     to dau-Betty Turpin
     wit;Jessee Lister,Thomas Beauchamp, Rebecca Fordred

                            f.131
DENNIS,John             1 Feb 1766          2 Sep 1767
     to son-Littleton, Real Estate. exec
     to wife-unnamed, balance. After death to
     son-John, son Littleton and dau.Sarah Holbrook w/o Thomas,
        dau-Leah Robertson,dau.Mary Pollitt
     to dau-Sarah Holbrook, that devised to her by my gr.dau.
        Elizabeth Hamilton
     to gr.ch-Samuel Handy,Mary Maddux,Elizabeth Handy,John
        Handy and William Handy, William Caldwell,Robert Caldwell,
        Mary Caldwell,Elizabeth Sanford
     wit;William Allen, John Broughton,Josiah Polk

                            f.131
GEDDES,Robert           5 Nov 1767          20 Nov 1767
     to son-William,exec.
     to son-Alexander Geddes of London
     to dau-Margaret Geddes of Philadelphia
     wit;Thomas Sloss,Andrew Francis Cheney,Samuel Wilson

                            f.131
WALLER,Thomas Sr.,planter   25 Apr 1762      18 Nov 1767
     to wife-Mary, tr. STEPPENY (desc.)and to my children,unnamed
     wit;Thomas Parramore,Margaret Grair,Joshua Parramore
     came;John Waller,made oath.

                            f.132
MERINE,William          28 Nov 1766          29 Dec 1767
     to son-William, 50a. LITTLE NECK
     to son-John, 100a. HUMPHRASSES
     to son-Matthew 50a.
     to sons-Charles and Zorobable,lands BAKERS FOLLY
     to daus-Jenitt and Ester
     wit;John Lankford,John Williams,Charity Williams

                            f.132-133
WILLIAMS,Thomas in old age  no.Jan 1768      16 Nov 1768
     to dau-Mary Bell and her children
     to gr.son-P,anner Williams,exec.,land where I live
     to gr.son-Thomas Williams,land where he lives, ½ marsh
        at Jeans Island called DIXONS LOTT
     to gr.son-David Williams,lands bou/o Major Day Scott on
        Wicomicco River. If no heirs to his brothers Planner,Thomas
     to gr.son-Levin Williams,land where he lives(Bounds his bro.
        Planner. and bounds Thomas King. 100a. marsh near Jeans Isld.
     to-Betty Turpin dau/o William
     wit;Outerbridge Horsey,Isaac Dixon,William Dixon
```

```
                              f.133
MADDOX,Alexander          11 Oct 1763        10 Feb 1768
    to wife-Elizabeth, 138a. of Manor plantation where I live
       after death to
    sons-Joseph,Zacarias,William
    to son-Alexander, 50a. on n/s of tr. WHITE FEALD
    to son-Zepheniah, 5a.
    to son-Ezekiah, 50a.
    to daus-Jenny Maddux,Sarah Hearn,Betty Maddox
    Benjamin Hearn,exec.
    wit;Isaac Maddox,Daniel Maddox,John Hitch

                              f.133
HITCH,Robert Sr.  -       9 Oct 1767         24 Mar 1768
    to eldest son-Isaac,dwelling plant.200a. HIGH SUFFOLK
    to sons Samuel and Nathan(under 15)be in care of Joseph
       Hitch Sr. and Joseph Hitch Jr.
    to-Joshua Bennett an orphan boy
    to wife-Eva, 1/3rds
    wit;William Handy,Joshua Hitch Sr.,Joseph Hitch Jr.

                              f.134
FRANSWAY,Benjamin of Pr.Anne 27 Feb 1768        16 Mar 1768
    to daus-Margaret and Mary Fransway of Nottingham, if
       living or to their children
    to-Mr. William Smith the Elder
    George Irving,Ephraim Wilson,Samuel Wilson,David  Wilson exect

                              f.134
CAVE,John                 16 Jan 1768         19 Feb 1768
    to wife-Anne, 100a.
    to son-Benjamin to care for my son William,bal. of lands
    wit;Hezekiah Read,James Read,Ester Read

                              f.134-135
ROBERTSON,James           5 Dec 1767          1 Apr 1768
    to dau-Mary 10a.
    to sons-John and James
    to wife-Mary,1/3rds
    to dau-unnamed
    wit;Isaac Taylor,William Badley,James Taylor

                              f.135
LONG,Randal,planter       27 Dec 1767         23 Feb 1768
    to mother-land where I live(desc.)adj. tr.COMEBY CHANCE.
       after her death to brother Samuel
    to brother-Jeffrey,balance of lands
    to brother-William
    to sisters-Sarah Long,Jean Beauchamp
    wit;William Cottingham,Thomas Cottingham,Shadrack Richardson

                              f.135-136
DASHIELL,George Sr.       3 Feb 1768          18 Mar 1768
    to wife-Rebeccah,exec.
    to dau-Sarah Walter, use of lands on Nanticoke where she
       lives. after death to gr.son.George Dashiell Walter
    to gr.dau.-Mary Nicholson d/o Joseph
    to gr.dau-Peggy Nicholson d/o Joseph,land Matthew Cannon
       deeded me being pt. of WHITTYS INVENTION. DEDFORD. Bal.
       of lands on Wicomico Riber. GEORGES MEADOW but if Nancy
       Mackmurray and Rebecca Mackmurray will pay charges I
       expended on GEORGES MEADOW to be their property.
    trustees-Jessee Dashiell,Isaac Hopins,George Dashiell
    wit;Matthew Cannon,John Collier,George Walter
```

BUTLER,Elizabeth   18 May 1766   16 Mar 1768
    to cousins-Stoughton Maddux, Lazarus Maddux
    to brother Lazarus's wife
    to cousins-Sarah Tull, Ann Maddux
    to cousin-Nelly Maddux d/o bro.Lazarus, she to pay her
      sister Betty 17pounds
    to-Ann Mary Hamon
    Samuel Tull,exec.
    wit;Joshua Hall,John Hall

COPE,David   –   31 Dec 1767   10 Feb 1768
    to mother-Margaret,lands
    to dau-Phebey Cope,dwelling plantation
    to sister-Sarah Cope
    to brother-John Cope,75a. where I live GREENS LOSS
    to wife-Sarah,exec.
    wit;William Wright,William Robertson,Mitchell Scott

COX,John of Stepney Parish 22 Oct 1765   30 Jun 1768
    to wife-unnamed
    to gr.dau.-Betty(Elizabeth)Jacobs, lot in Princess Anne
      town #12 and #13
    to-Thomas Conoly and to his wife my dau.Margaret
    to gr.son-Thomas Cox
    to-Benjamin Dashiell,Jessee Dashiell, Isaac Hopkins,
      to be trustees to gr.dau.Betty Jacobs
    wit;Sarah Dashiell,Rebekah Whithear,Susannah Dashiell

WILSON,George,planter   14 Mar 1768   5 Apr 1768
    to son-William,tr. where he lives SECURITY (desc.) bounds
    DIXONS LOTT
    to gr.son-George Wilson s/o Wm. to inherit above lands
    to wife-Roday,exec.
    to son-Abraham,bal. of lands afsd. if no issue to son David
    to sons-Jessee exec., and Levin
    to brother-Samuel Wilson
    to daus-Sophia,Sarah,Hannah,Ann, Mary Wilson
    wit;Purnell Outten,Joseph Wilson,David Pryer

FRANCES WILSON   10 Sep 1760   4 Jul 1768
    to sons-George Irving,John Irving,execs.
    to gr.sons-Daniel,John and George Wailes
    to daus-Mary Spence,Ann Irving, Bridget Dashiell
    to gr.daus.-Margaret Spence,Mary Irving d/o John,Eleanor
      Irving d/o George, Eleanor Dashiell,Mary Spence,Betty Irvin
    wit;Thomas Sloss,Robert Jones

TATUM,John of Stepney Parish 10Oct 1767   23 Jun 1768
    to wife-Elizabeth,exec.
    to gr.son-Robert Persons
    to dau-Elizabeth Wright
    wit;Aaron Speer,Jacob Speer,Henry Speer

```
                              f.138
DORMAN,John              4 Oct 1768            1 Nov 1768
.    to son-John, dwelling plantation 139 3/4a.
     to sons-Zadock and Matthias
     to dau-Mary
     to wife-Catherine,exec.
     to son-Matthias, to be bound to William Robbins. He
        to be advised by Nehemiah Tilghman,Gideon Tilghman
     wit;William Taylor,Michael Cluff,Gideon Tilghman

                              f.139
GASTENEAU,George Lewis,Schoolmaster,14 Dec 1763 31 Oct 1768
     to wife-Mary, 1/3rds and plantation,exec.
     to son-Job, plantation CHANCE 100a.,exec.
     to daus-Elizabeth and Mary (under 18),Jane Russell,
        Tabitha Messick
     wit;Thomas Stanford,John Reed, Sarah Reed

                              f.139-140
WALKER,Thomas Sr.        6 Apr 1766            3 Sep 1768
     to wife-Betty. exec.
     to sons-Thomas Jr.,James,William,Charles,Jessee
     to daus-Mary Taylor, Betty Walker
     to son-Mark,50a. TARKILL GLADE
     to son-Emmanuel,50a. on Cod Creek WALKERS FOLLY
     to son-Henry, Dwelling plantation. 110a.
     wit;Aaron Speer,Isabelle Walter,Betty Walter

                              f.140
BOSTON,Esau              2 Jun 1768            30 Aug 1768
     to-William Wood, tr. NAN ELLESSES RIDGE,he to pay for.
     to gr.sons-Elijah and Isaac sons of Matthew Boston(under20)
     to son-Jacob,exec.
     to gr.sons-Esau, Jacob sons of Jacob Boston
     to dau-Mary Cottingham
     to gr.daus-Mary Cottingham d/o John, Betty Boston
     to son-Lazarus
     to gr.son-Jacob son of Esau Boston
     to gr.sons-Elijah,Isaac,Ephraim,David Boston
     trustee, Capt. Thomas Hayward
     wit;Purnell Outten,William Cearsly,Isaac Marshall

                              f.140-141
JONES,Thomas            23 Apr 1768            20 Sep 1768
     to wife-Elizabeth,exec.
     to children-Ann, John Britain,Margaret,Richard and
        Joshua Jones (all under 13)
     Friend-Thomas Dashiell to advise family
     wit;John Parker,James Done

                              f.141
DREADON,Jonathan,Planter  3 Feb 1769          23 Mar 1769
     to wife-Rachel,exec.
     to son-Thomas, 50a. POWELLS CHANCE
     to children-unnamed
     wit;John Thomson,Hamilton Dreadon,John Blain
     came;John Tull made oath
```

```
                          f.141-142
HARRIS,Richard            24 Oct 1766        21 Mar 1769
     to dau-Junise Harris,dwelling plantation HARRIS LOTT
     to dau-Mary Hufinton
     Solomon Harris,exec.
     wit;James West,George Harris,Sarah West

                          f.142
ADAMS,Hope,planter        5 Sep 1768         13 Dec 1768
     to son-Hope, pt. 2 trs.MITCHELLS ADVENTURE, GOOD HOPE
       (desc.) if no issue to my son Samuel,exec.
     to sons-Phillip, Nathan,David
     to wife-Sarah, 1/3rds
     to daus-Sarah Adams, Edeliah Dakes
     wit;William Morre,Jacob Addams Sr.,Thomas Moore

                          f.142-143
SHORES,William            16 Feb 1768        14 Feb 1769
     to dau-Mary Shores,negro left by her gr.father Joseph Ward
     to daus-Alce and Sarah
     to son-John
     wife's brother Stephen Ward, exec.
     wit; Gowan Wright,John Phebus Sr.John Martain

                          f.143
COLLINS,John              8 Nov 1768         23 Jan 1769
     to eldest son-Samuel,plantation where I live
     to son-Stephen,lands pur/o Joshua Dickerson
     to dau-Rebeccah Collins  (all ch.under age)
     to wife-Abigail (now pregnant)
     wit;Littleton Dennis,Caleb Milbourn,Jacob Adams

                          f.143-144
DASHIELL,Mitchell         22 Dec 1768        31 Jan 1769
     to dau-Ann Buchanan w/o James
     to dau-Eunice Wailes w/o John
     to sons-Charles and Benjamin
     to son-George,dwelling plantation. Lands on Rewastico left
       me by my father PHARSALIA, tr.GOOD LUCK, if no issue to
     son-Robert, tr. LONG POINT
     to wife-Mary
     wit;Joseph Scroggin,Joseph Venables, George Low

                          f.144
GREEN,Richard,planter     27 Dec 1768        10 Jan 1769
     to son-Samuel, tr. MARYS CHANCE
     to son-Isaac, tr. GREENS LUCK,except 33 1/3a.to son John
     to son-Ezekiel Green,manor plantation. 90a. bou/o James
       West, GREENS RECANTATION
     to son-John,small lot s/s MARYS CHOICE. land obtained in a
       resurvey with Lazarus Huffington
     Son-Isaac to satisby debts due to Jonathan Bounds and Ruth
       Dickerson for bond of Samuel Jackson and John Anderson.
       To ppy debt due William Moore.  exec.
     wit;William Moore,William Dorman,Thomas Humphries

                          f.145
POTTER,Henry,planter      8 Apr.1769         2 May 1769
     to my now wife-Mary,exec.
     to daus-Betty Potter,Sarah Matthews,Rachel Adams
     to son-Henry
     to son-Thomas Wood Potter,exec.
     wit;Elijah Conway,Levi Adams,David Adams
```

f.145
LAWES,Panter   20 Jan 1769   5 Apr 1769
    to wife-Mary,plantation where I live. 1/3rds. exec
    to son-William, 100a. in Little Neck Creek
    to sons-Gilbert, Thomas,John
    to daus-Nanney, Betty
    wit;Levin Dashiell,Benjamin Sasser,William Waller

f.146
RELPH,William,planter   21 Feb 1766   26 Apr 1769
    to-Joseph Parremore,25a. out of GOOD LUCK AT LAST out
        of 150a. near Black Water. He to pay for said land.
    to son-Mitchel, pt. afsd.lands
    to son-George, bal. afsd tracts.
    to sons-William(exec.),Thomas, John
    to wife-Sarah
    to daus-Rachel, Sarah
    wit;John Williams, Charity Williams,John Williams Jr.

f.146
SPEER,Henry   19 Jul 1758   7 Aug 1769
    to son-Andrew, dwelling plantation BILLESHINE 100a.,
        pt. DONNE GOALL 200a.(desc.) exec.
    to dau-Jean Speer
    wit;John Wales,Cornelius English,Jacob Giles

f.146-147
DASHIELL,Rebeccah   24 Dec 1768   27 Jun 1769
    to sons-John Stuart, William Stuart(exec.)
    to gr.dau-Rebecca Porter
    to dau-Betty Wales
    to gr.sons-James, Haist and Daniel Porter
    to-gr.daus-Rebeccah Mackmorey, Ann Russell
    to-Sarah Porter
    wit;John Shiles,Major Shiles

f.147
HITCH,John --   30 Jul 1767   10 Aug 1769
    to wife-Isable
    wit;Nehemiah Hitch,Charles Nicholson

f.147-148
ADAMS,Alexander   27 Apr 1769   26 Sep 1769
    to-Sarah Adams wid/o dec'd son Alexander, pt.four tr.s
        WALLISSES CHANCE, WIDSOR,TROUBLE,DENTRY on road from
        Wicomico Creek to Pr.Anne town, and to her children
    to gr.son-Alexander Adams s/o Alexander afsd.lands
    to son-William, lands adj. afsd.(desc.)
    to son-John,bal.of lands. two tr.sGLASGOW SWAMP, WILSONS FOLLY
    to son-Andrew, 2 trs.TURKEY TRAP RIDGE,CLOVER GROUND
    to gr.son-Alexander s/o son Samuel, tr.above Hustons Mill
        in Worc.Co. BEARFIELDS
    wit;Charles Paterson,Jessee Dorman,David Crouch

f.148
BANKS,Robert   2 Sep 1768   23 Nov 1769
    to wife-Mary,lands on s/s Wicomico River
    to dau-Ann Carrey
    to son-Isiah, tr. HALLS ADVENTURE on n/s Wicomico where he live
    to son-Robert, pt. tr. ROBERTS SECURITY between Wicomicco River
        and Disheroons branch.
                                                cont'd.

BANKS,Robert,cont'd
    to son-Thomas,pt. ROBERTS SECURITY (desc.)
    to son-Henry,lands bou/o David Howard HOWARDS DISCOVERY
      and BRITAIN
    wit;Francis Chittam,William Melone,William Murray

                f.148-149
GILES,Thomas,planter   6 Oct 1769   22 Nov 1769
    to wife-Ann, 1/3rds.
    to son-Jacob,pt. tr. GILES LOTT on road from Wicomicco
      Ferry to Broad Creek, where he lives 125a.
    to son-Thomas,his dwelling plant,s/s afsd tr. 125a.
    to son-Isaac, my dwelling plantation
    to son-Williamplantation where he lives(desc.),exec.
    to son-John (if he returns home)
    to daus-Ann and Sarah
    wit;Thomas Moore,George Wailes,William Tully

                f.149
BALEY,George   23 Sep 1769   31 Aug 1770
    to wife-Newton(may be pregnant)
    to sons-Elais Baley,Robins Baley, Obed,Benjamin,George,Littleton
    to daus-Anna,Sarah,Newton
    wit;Samuel Adams,William Bailey,Charles Patterson

                f.149-150
CORDREY,Rachel   18 Mar 1770   7 Jun 1770
    to son-Nicholas Evans Collier,tr. mortgaged by David
      Cordrey and myself to Col.Levin Gale. exec.
    to gr.son-George Collier
    to gr.dau-Priscilla Collier
    to daus-Ailes Harris,Jane Anderson
    (wishes to be burried by 1st.husband(unnamed)
    wit;George Day Scott,John Patterson

                f.150
HAYMAN,Isaac   28 Feb 1770   20 Jun 1770
    to son-Joshua,exec.,s/end two trs.WOLFS PITT RIDGE,ADDITION,
      (desc.ments.path to my brother Charles Hayman's)
    to son-Isaac,bal.afsd trs.
    to wife-Leddy,exec.
    wit;Mills Bayley,William Redden,Stephen Redden

                f.150-151
RICHARDSON,Benjamin   16 May 1755   15 May 1770
    to wife-Sarah,exec.
    to-Elizabeth Fletcher,John Fletcher,George Fletcher,James
      Fletcher,Levin Fletcher,children-in-law.
    wit;Hugh Henry,Thomas Langford
    15 May 1770 came James Vance,made oath that the Sunday before
    Thomas Langford died and said Langford told him that he was
    at Benjamin Richardsons to borrow money and was a witness to
    the will land that Mr.Hugh Henry wrote it.
    14 Jun.1770,came Benjamin Langford who heard his father say
    (now dead) that he was a wit. to above will and verifies
    Thomas Langfords signature. (both wit.dec'd at probate)
    Came;Joseph Scroggin,Thomas Fletcher,Samuel Wilson made oath,
    verifies handwritting of the Rev.Hugh Henry.

WALSTON,Boaz   f.151
                               18 Mar 1770   16 Oct 1770
     to son-Joy,dwelling plantation,exec.
     to daus-Deborough Roach,Ebey McDaniel,Rebecca Hammon
     to sons-John and Jessee
     wit;Randall Revell, P.Taylor,Ezekiel West

CALLOWAY,John Sr.   f.151-152
                               25 Jan 1770   6 Mar 1771
     to dau-Rachel and her child Mary Lynch
     to gr.son-Levi Calloway(under 21)
     to daus-Sarah,Catherine,Ann
     to son Ebenezer,dwelling plantation,exec.
     to sons-Edward,John and Isaac
     wit;William Horsey,Francis Godard,John Cordray

WRIGHT,Zebulon   f.152
                               24 Jan 1770   27 Feb 1771
     to wife-Suffiah,exec.
     to brother Stephen
     to child-Betty(under 16)
     Thomas Humphris to oversee
     wit;John Anderson,Sarah Dorman,Sarah Shurman

WILLIN,Thomas Sr.of Stepney Parish,yoeman
                               13 Feb 1770   22 Feb 1771
     to dau-Elizabeth McIntire,25a. marsh out of Isaac Handy's
       pasture
     to son-John Jr.,50a. marsh,adj.afsd
     to son-Thomas and son-Robert
     to gr.son-Levin Willin
     friend-Isaac Atkinson,exec. and trustee
     to wife-Elizabeth Willin and her two sons,Littleton Willin
       and Leonard Willin
     wit;Aaron Speer,Charles Hammond,William Frazier

TREHEARN,James   f.153
                               28 Aug 1769   23 Mar 1771
     to son-Samuel,lands
     to son-Cyrus
     to daus-Betty Trehearn,Glepora Silbet
     to wife-Ann
     wit;Nehemiah Turpin,Coulbourn Long,Benjamin Scott

KINNEY,William,planter   f.153
                               12 May 1660   13 Jun 1771
     to son-William, tr. KENNYS CHANCE, GOOD NEIGHBORHOOD, pt.of
       DESARTE(desc.),dwelling plantation. if no heirs to
     son-Joseph, pt. of DESARTE, exec.
     to dau-Ann
     wit;James Windsor,John Young,George Bacon
     came-Mary Kinney widow,demands 1/3rds

WILLS,Benjamin   f.154
                               17 April1770   4 Sep 1771
     to wife-Sarah,dwelling plantation, after death to
     son-Benjamin
     to son-Lazarus
     to daus-Sarah and Mary
     Joshua Ellis to raise boys Benjamin and Lazarus
     to son-Isaac
     Bal. to Richard Knowles Sr. to pay my debts.
     wit;James Haynie,Patience Knowles,Magdalene Ellis

```
                                   f.154
STEPHENS,William          18 Dec 1769        21 Mar 1771
     to eldest dau.-Hester Mills
     to daus-Betty and Sarah Stephens
     to sons-Benjamin,George,William
     to son-Levi,dwelling plantation and lands
     to wife-Margaret
     wit;Joseph Hitch Jr.Joshua Hitch,Risdon Nicholson
                                   f.154-155
TULL,Esther               15 Feb 1770        21 Mar 1771
     to son-John,exec.,negro now in poss. of Stephen Tull
     to gr.daus-Rodah Tull,Sophia Wharton & Esther Tull d/o Joshua
     to gr.son-Edward Beauchamp
     to son-Joshua and son Stephen
     to gr.children-Esther,Sarah,Betty,Levi ch/o Stephen Tull
     wit;Charles Hall,John Lawes,Thomas Tull
                                   f.155
FULLERTON,Mary            30 Jun 177;        26 Jul 1771
     to gr.daus-Peggy and Mary Fullerton
     to sons-John,Charles,Joshua,Tubman
     wit;John Watkins,Rachel Owens, Lave Anderson
                                   f.155-6
COLEBURN,Rachel of Coventry Parish 22 Dec 1770 27 Sep 1771
     to son-Isaac,exec.
     to gr.son-Sewill Dreadon
     to daus-Ann Coleburn,Grace Beauchamp w/o Marcy
     to sons-Benajmin, Solomon
     to dau-Jane Dreadon w/o Samuel
     to gr.dau- Rachel Handy Coleburn
     to gr.son-William Coleburn s/o William
     wit;George Tull,George Guillett
                                   f.156
KILLUM,John               6 Jun 1771         17 Jul 1771
     to son-Edward,plantation where I live on Nanticoke River.
        Pt. two trs. ARTHER LOW, LARGE. CHERRY TREE ISLAND,exec.
     to daus-Ezabel Dashiell w/o Robert,Margaret Killum,Sarah
        Handy,Priscilla Killum
     to gr.sons-William Kellum,Nicholas Kellum
     to gr.daus-Sarah and Ann Kellum
     to wife-Sarah
     blanance of lands to be sold
     wit;John Piper,John Weatherly,Henry Acworth
                                   f.156-157
BURT,Joseph              26 Aug 1770         9 Sep 1771
     formerly of Hunterdon County in West Jersey
     to bro-in-law-Moses Read,land and mills in Cumberland
        Co.Pennsylvania
     to brother-Richard Burt,exec.
     to sisters-Margaret,Elizabeth,Sarah and Deborah
     wit;Samuel Wilson,William Mackey,John Winder
                                   f.157
DORMAN,Michael           1 Oct 1769          10 Sep 1771
     to son-John,pt. tr.DORMANS CONCLUSION(desc.)on road from
        Wicomico Creek to Priness Anne Town
     to son-Jesse, trs. GULLETTS HOPE, ST.PETERS HILL
     to son-Isaiah,exec.,lands(desc.)bounds John Jones & DORMANS
        DISCOVERY
     to wife-Mary, 1/3rds. exec.                    cont'd.
```

DORMAN,Michael,cont'd
        to dau-Elizabeth
        to son-Chase,exec.,balance DORMANS DISCOVERY,DORMANS
            CONCLUSION,GOLDEN QUARTER, NELSONS CHOICE
        to sons-Michael and Solomon
        wit;Matthias Miles,Isaac Newman,Thomas Newman

                         f.157-158
DASHIELL,Thomas   13 May 1771   26 Aug 1771
        to son-William,lands
        to daus-Henny Dashiell,Patience and Jane Dashiell
        to friend-Susannah Guibert
        Friend-William Allen of Worc.Co. and Patience his wife,gdns.
        brother-George Dashiell,exec. guardian or Littleton Dennis
            of Worc.Co. gdn.
        wit;Robert Malone,Peter Malone,William Malone

                         f.158-159
WARD,James,planter   20 Oct 1770   21 Nov 1770
        to wife-Rachel,plantation where I live, afterdeath to
        son- Thomas,lands
        to sons-William,Jessee(exec.)and Starling(exec.)
        to daus-Sarah Ward,Mary Killum
        to gr.dau-Hannah Moor
        to-William Wheatley and Thomas Moor
        wit;William Miles, Stephen Ward,John Cullen

                         f.159
WHITE,Thomas   1 Dec 1766   21 Nov 1770
        to cousin-Abram Outten,tr. where I live ADAMS GARDEN
        to wife-Sarah,exec., tr. LITTLEWORTH
        wit;Purnell Outten,Henry Cohoon,Henry Potter,Wm.Adams

                         f.159
TREHEARN,Ann,noncupative will 22 Oct 1770   17 Dec 1770
        estate to Elizabeth Trehearn and Sires(Cyrus)Trehearn
        wit;Nehemiah Turpin,Benjamin Scott

                         f.160
XPHER(Christopher)DOWDALL   none   20 Nov 1771
        to wife-Sarah and to William Pollitt
        wit;Joshua Polk,William Strawbridge

                         f.160
NAIRNE,James,Sr.,planter   3 Oct 1767   11 Jun 1771
        to son-James,exec.plantation in Indian Town,if no heirs to
        male heirs of my dau.Isabell
        to gr.son-James Nairne Harper(under 21)
        to dau-Peggy Harper and daus.Isabell Mackneider,Eleanor Nairne
        wit;Isaac Dickeson,Jacob Addams,William Hall

                         f.161
TURPIN,William   10 Sep 1771   28 Sep 1771
        to son-Denwood,dwelling plantation. tr. HAWTREE
        to gr.son-William after decease of son Denwood, afsd.lands
        to gr.sons-John Turpin,Denwood Turpin,William Ballard, James
            Ballard
        to dau-Priscillah Ballard
        son-Denwood to take Elizabeth McClemeys son Woney until of age
        to gr.dau-Mary Turpin
        wit;Stephen Horsey,William Fountain,Whittey Turpin

f.161-162
DULANY,Paul, planter   6 Mar 1773   19 Apr 1773
 to son-Henry,dwelling plantation where I live,pt.comming
  to me out of Benjamin Byrds Jr's estate(under age)
 to brothe-John Dulany
 Father-Dennis Dulany,exec.
 wit;Benjamin Lunby,John Goddard,Mathias Vinson
 came;Mary Dulaney widow,demands 1/3rds

f.162
ROBERTS(Grandee)Rencher   3 Jan 1773   24 Jun 1773
 livingin Dam Quarter,planter.
 to son-John Roberts alias Grandee,100a s/s Rockwalking River
 to son-Rencher alias Grandee,50a. on Wicomico near plantation
  of Marshall Smith, THOMASES LOTT
 to daus-Betty Martin, Sarah Roberts
 to wife-Mary
 wit;John Kelly Sr.Thomas Roberts,Bartholomew Roberts

f.162-163
KING,John   11 Oct 1773   7 Dec 1773
 to son-Whittington,tr.CHANCE,FRIENDS ADVICE, tr.taken up in
  the name of Jarvis Ballard called BALLARD. KINGS LOTT, 29a. tr.
  that bounds HAZARD and Rev.Hamilton Bell.
 Land on s/s Manokin River now in possession of Thomas and
  William Walstone to be sold
 to wife-Ann,1/3rds,exec.
 to children-John,Leah,Benjamin
 Isaac Holland,Denwood Wilson,George Wilson to advise family
 wit;David Wilson,John Law,Levin Wilson

f.163-164
SMITH,Margaret   24 Jan 1772   29 Jun 1773
 to gr.son-Edward Smith,dwelling plantation,lands,exec.
 to gr.dau-Rebeccah Smith
 to son-William
 wit;Stephen Mitchell,John Puzey,Mary Mitchell Jr.

f.164-165
MITCHELL,Isaac   26 Apr 1773   22 Jun 1773
 to eldest son-John,two trs.in Worc.Co. QUACOSSON,BEACH RIDGE
 to son-Josiah,tr. in Worc.Co. HOG YARD 170a.
 to son-James, tr.ADDITION TO GOOD SUCESS 266a, tr.NEIGHBOURS
  NEGLEST 80a. in Som.Co.,MITCHELLS DISCOVERY(desc.)
 to son-Joshua,tr. MIDDLESEX 250a.,pt.WILLIAMS HOPE 62½a.,
  land pur/o Jonathan Tull. Bal.MITCHELLS DISCOVERY
 to wife-Jane,exec.
 to son-in-law-Samuel Adams
 to daus-Mary,Jany,Betty Mitchell
 wit;Elias White,Isaac Costen,William Stephens

f.165
WOOD,Ann   25 Jan 1773   9 Mar 1773
 to son-Elijah and son William
 to daus-Leah Wood exec.,Martha Wood,Sary Hall
 wit;Sary Taylor,William Moore,Isaac Addams

```
                              f.165-166
WOOD,Levi                 19 Jan 1772          9 Mar 1773
     to sister-Leah Wood,exec.,tr.DUBLIN. If no issue to
     Levi Wood son of Elijah
     to sister-Martha,land ALLENS CONTEST
     to mother-Ann Wood
     to brother-Elijah, note due from William Hall
     to-William Hall
     wit;William Moore,Isaac Adams

                              f.166-167
SCROGIN,Joseph             5 Sep 1772          27 Feb 1773
     to son-John Scrogin,exec.,two trs.FAIRFIELDS 129a.,ADDITION
        TO FAIRFIELDS 84½a. except 37a.adj. that I have given bond f⊂
     to Elijah Hearne
     to son-Joseph,tr. STANCE 150a.
     to son-Samuel, tr. ANYTHING 100a.
     to son-Robert, tr. HAZZARD 105a.,exec.
     to dau-Ann Caldwell Scrogin
     to sons-Phillip Jenkins Scrogin,Thomas Clark Scrogin
     to daus-Sarah,Betty,Milley,Anne,Mathilda
     wit;Richard Waller,Ebenezer Waller,Hezekiah Maddux

                              f.167
DISHAROON,Josephus        10 Jan 1773          9 Feb 1773
     to-Nuton Disharoon,land in Som.Co. 200a.(under 21)
     to mother-Mary
     to-Michale Disheroon s/o Constant
     to-Ann Sterling Banks
     to 4 sisters(unnamed) and brother Constant,exec.
     wit;Stephen Adams,Frances Disharoon,Henry Banks

                              f.167-168
DISHEROON,Thomas          28 Oct 1772          9 Feb 1773
     to brother Obediah's son Stephen
     to brother-Francis Disheroon,dwelling plantation,exec.
     to sister-Isbell Disheroon(under 16)
     wit;Stephen Roach,George Disheroon

                              f.168
SURMAN(Shearman)Mary      14 Feb 1772          17 Mar 1773
     to sister-Betty Surman,bond from John Anderson
     to sister-Leah Surman
     to brother-Nehemiah Surman
     to aunts-Sarah Anderson,Margaret Anderson
     to uncle-John Anderson,exec.
     wit;Isaac Green,John Anderson Jr.

                              f.169
BANKS,Thomas              9 Dec 1771           17 Mar 1773
     to brother Henry,all left me at my fathers death,that to be
        left me by me mother if I never return
     wit;Daniel Walker(wrote above will.)

                              f.169
VAUGHAN,Ephraim          22 Mar 1773          17 Aug 1773
     to son-William,150a.pt. tr.COXES DISCOVERY devised me by my
        father William Vaughan my now dwelling plantation.
     to son-Levin,150a.,100a. bou/o Thomas Kennady being pt. of
        COXES DISCOVERY, 50a. ISLAND GLADE
     to son-James,50a. POPLAR RIDGE. if no heir to Ephraim Caughn
     to son-Jonathan, an improvement where Sarah Rhoads now lives
     to wife-Betty, 1/3rds,exec.
     wit;Caleb Balding,Jethro Vaughn,Charles Moore
                              50
```

```
                              f.170
WILLIN,Thomas Jr.           4 Mar 1773          24 Mar 1773
     to son-George,2a. out of HOG QUARTER,exec.
     to son-Levin,bal.afsd tr.HOG YARD. WILLINS LOT
     to wife-Priscillah
     to son-Samuel(under 21)lands
     to bro-in-law-Daniel McIntyre
     to sons-Matthias and Thomas
     to son-in-law-Charles Hammond
     wit;John Willin,James Willin,John M arshall

                              f.170-171
TULL,Solomon                20 Jul 1769          6 Jul 1773
     to son-Solomon,dwelling plantation, exec.
     wit;William Fountain,Collier Fountain,Whitty Turpin

                              f.171-172
WHITTINGTON,Southy          20 Feb 1770          17 Mar 1773
     to son-Southy,lands already in his possession,exec.
     to wife-Mary
     to sons-Stevenson, William
     to gr.dau-Mary Cox
     to son-Isaac, tr. ADDITION, tr.CHANCE, marsh RECOVERY 130a.
     Friend-George Hayward Esq. of Worc.Co. tr.CHOICE on e/s
        Nasaongo Creek in Worc.Co. at Indian Town
     wit;Elijah Coulbourn,Jeffrey Long,Samuel Long

                              f.172
BALLARD,Anne relic of Jarvis 19 Nov 1772         9 Feb 1773
     to sons-Jarvis,Arnold,Charles,William
     to daus-Sarah Bowen,Mary Ballard
     to gr.dau-Mary Read
     wit;Andrew Francis.Cheney,Esther Foscue,Elinor Martin

                              f.172-173
HITCH,Elgate                19 Mar 1772          9 Feb 1773
     to wife-Rachel,house where I live, 1/3rds
     to gr.son-William Elgate Hitch(under 21)lands (desc.) bounds
        William Handys, that his father gave to him.  A house
        I built for my son Joshua, if no issue to
     son-Robert. bal. of lands,exec.
     to gr.daus-Mary and Elizabeth Hitch(under 16)
     wit;Stephen Garland,Joshua Byrd,Thomas Byrd

                              f.173
KNIGHT,James                6 Nov 1771 -         27 Jan 1773
     to son-Nehemiah
     to wife-Elizabeth,exec.
     to dau-Betty Barklet
     to daus-Mary,Martha,Sarah,Tabitha 160a. on Nanticoke River
     wit;Patrick McCaley,William Wright,Richard Bradley

                              f.173-174
PRIOR,Ann                   19 Dec 1772          26 Jan 1773
     to son-Randolph, tr. MATIS ENJOYMENT, tr.CONCCLUSION,exec.
     to son-David
     wit;Sampson Wheatly,Killiam Lankford,Samuel Trehearn
```

51

```
                              f.174-175
GILES,William               26 Jan 1772          5 Apr 1773
      to-Easter Dunkin,50a. GILES VENTER on rd.from Quantico
         Mill to Rewastico Mill
      to-Ephraim King and his son Samuel
      to-Leah Dunkin,50a. pt.GILES FOLLY surveyed by Samuel
         Jackson. 58a. marsh includes island GREAT OAK ISLAND, pt.
         tr. LARGEE first surveyed by James Givans. 10a. and water
         mill pt. of ELIZABETHS CHOICE & MARYS CHOICE and resurveyed
         as GREENS LUCK
      to-Catherine Dunkin, Margaret Dunkin,Elendor Kemp
      to-Solomon Harris, 58a. pt. of LARGEE
      to-sister-Mary Harris, bal. of GILES FOLLY (desc.)
      to-William Giles Jr., 150a. SALLOPE
      to-Isaac Giles,Jacob Giles,John Harris,William Harris
      to-Unicy Lumley
      friend-John Harris,exec.
      wit;Matthew Kemp,Samuel Jackson,George Bennett,Josiah Phillips
```

```
                              f.175-176
RICHARDSON,John             13 Jun 1751         16 Jul 1773
      to wife-Mary and to my children(unnamed)
      wit;Hanah Trahearn,James Trahearn,Benjamin Cottman
```

```
                              f.176
SURMAN,Joshua               26 Mar 1773          2 Apr 1773
      to brothers-Isaac and Edward Surman
      to-David Ragling,exec.
      to-Samuel Mores 40ah. for use of his daughter
      to-Mary Neàl and Mary Mores Jr.
      wit;James Bounds,Thomas Collins
```

```
                              f.176-177
ACWORTH,Temperance           8 Feb 1773         29 Mar 1773
      to gr.son-Charles s/o James Acworth (under 21)
      to sons-Charles, and Train exec.
      to gr.sons-Thomas,James and William Acworth
      wit;John Phillips,James West
```

```
                              f.177-178
WHEATLY,Sampson              2 Jun 1773         20 Nov 1773
      to now wife,Mary,lands,exec.
      to dau-Mary
      to dau-Betty,lands after wife's death WHEATTLEYS DIFFICULT
         PURCHASE, tr.FRISH GROVE, MERCHANTS TREASURE,GREEN FIELD,
         WHEATLEYS SECOND ADDITION,PRIVILEDGE,LITTLE WORTH,NEW
         BOSTON,DAMM SWAMP and tr.bou/o Thomas Adams 70a. pt.of
         ADAMS CHANCE
      to brother-William Wheatly
      wit;Elijah Coulbourn,Isaac Whittington,John Truitt
```

```
                              f.178
OTLY,Coventon               27 Oct1773         17 Nov 1773
      to mother-Martha Cox
      wit;Thomas Layfield,Jacob Milbourn,Rachel Cullin
```

```
                              f.179
DICKESON,Isaac              19 Mar 1771         19 Oct 1773
      towife-Cateron,dwelling plantation, after death to
      son-James,afsd and tr. bou/o George Dickeson MORRISSES HOPE
      to daus-Sarah and Rachel
      to sons-Peter,Joshua,Levi
      wit;Durnell Outten,Jessee Hall,Isaac White
```

TAYLOR,William   10 Mar 1770   19 Oct 1773
    to son-James,170a. out of ROUND POND
    to son-Abraham,117a. out of ROUND POND, where he now lives
    to son-Isaac, bal. of afsd.land
    to wife-Sarah
    to gr.son-William Taylor
    to son-James Taylor's children
    to gr.dau-Phillip Taylor
    to daus-Ann Moor,Betty Wailes,Mary Hitch
    to gr.ch-Thomas Moor,William Wailes,Betty Hitch
    wit;Charles Moor,John Roberson,Richard Badley

f.180

DASHIELL,Anna of Stepney Parish 21 Mar 1773   15 Apr 1773
    to sons-Matthias,Arthur,William, lands
    to daus-Jane and Milcah
    James Robertson,gdn. andexec.
    wit;Ephraim Stevens,Samuel Collins Adams,Nancy Dixon

f.181-182

TOADVINE, Thomas   22 Aug 1771   23 Jun 1772
    to son-Stephen,exec.,pt. tr.TOADVINES MILL(desc.)
    to son-Arnall,exec.,bal.afsd.tr., TOADVINES SECURITY
    to dau-Mary
    Friends-Isaiah Banks and George Disheroon, guardians
    wit;Jonathan Knight,John Christopher,Ebenezer Waller

f.182-183

HOPKINS,John   25 Mar 1771   6 Jul 1772
    to sisters-Elizabeth and Grace Hopkins
    to brother Stephen,exec.
    wit;Aaron Mezick,Nehemiah Crockett

f.183

WOOLFORD,Charles   1 May 1772   21 Jul 1772
    to son-Thomas,lands, if no heirs to
    son-John, lands(desc.)200a. If no heir to
    sons-William Pitt Woolford, Tubman Woolford
    to wife-Mary Ann, 1/3rds
    wit;Thomas G.Denwood,James Wilson,John Winder

f.184

WILSON,David   15 May 1772   29 Jul 1772
    living at head of Barren Creek
    to son-John,dwelling plantation. If no heirs to
    daus-Elizabeth and Denny Wilson
    to son-Ephraim, other ½ lands. If no heirs to
    daus-Ann,Polly and Ellenor Wilson
    to wife-Ellener, 1/3rds.,exec.
    wit;Joseph Venables,William Gravenor,Thomas Gravenor

f.184-185

PHILLIPS,James   14 Dec 1770   5 Mar 1772
    to wife-Sarah,lands,exec.
    to gr.son-James Phillips Wheatly
    to gr.daus-Esther Joyns alias Wheatly, Elizabeth Wheatly,
        Ann Wheatly
    to gr.sons-William and Johnson Wheatly
    wit;John Roberson,Levin Huffington,Thomas Huffington

```
                            f.185-186
LONG,Solomon                1 Oct 1765          10 Jul 1772
     to son-David,100a.ADVENTURE near mouth of Manokin River,
        tr.SAMPIRE 130a. adj.
     to son-Solomon,dwelling plantation AMITY 260a., 15a. bou/o
        Peter Spencer Hack
     to son-in-law-Joseph Ward
     to wife-Margaret,exec.
     to wife's sister-Sarah Maddux
     to sons-William and Zadock
     to daus-Jane w/o John Hayward, Matilda Long,Elizabeth,Sarah,
        and Rebeccah Long
     wit;Jessee King,Thomas Jones,Thomas Mitchell,John King

                            f.186-187
LINDSEY,Thomas,planter 9 Jul 1765             20 Nov 1771
     to son-David,dwelling plantation,exec.
     to daus-Sarah,Priscilla,Leah
     to son-Francis
     wit;Purnell Outten,Elijah Conner,Shadrack Outten

                            f.187-188
GILLIS,Levin                17 Jun 1772         3 Aug 1772
     to wife-Sarah,1/3rds.exec.
     to sons-Thomas and Levin,lands bounds the Wading place at
        head of Wicomico Creek.GILLISSES RUN (desc.)bounds
        Andrew Adam's and Eden Free School
     to daus-Mary and Sarah
     to son-Levin
     to brother-Joseph Gillis
     to gr.children-Levin Piper andLeah Piper
     wit;John Adams,Samuel Collins Adams,Andrew Adams

                            f.188
DISHAROON,John of Accoc.Co.Va. 20 May 1772      19 Aug 1772
     to brother-Josephus Disheroon,exec.,land in Som.Co. 200a.
     to-Nuton Disheroon(under 21)and Obediah Disheroon
     to brother-Constant Disheroon,exec.
     to four sisters,(unnamed)
     wit;William Selby,Elijah Milbourn,Thomas Sanford

                            f.188-189
COVINGTON,Thomas            17 Oct 1765         9 Nov.1771
     to brother-Samuel,estate,exec. If no issue to
     Aunt Martha Holbrook
     wit;Elisha Warwick,John Holbrook

                            f.189-190
HOPKINS,Stephen            24 Aug 1770          8 Jan 1772
     to wife-Elizabeth
     to son-Stephen,land on Nanticoke(desc.)being pt.of WARE
     to third son-Robert, lands (desc.) SAND ISLAND
     to 5th son-Richard,exec.,lands, MULBURY ISLAND
     to 4th son-Charles,lands. To Charles and Stephen CAGES ISLAND
     To gr.son-Stephen Hopkins
     to gr.daus-Elizabeth Hopkins,Grace  Hopkins,Jean Hopkins
        alias Hickman
     to daus-Ann Hopkins alias Mezick,Elizabeth Hopkins alias
        Wedzer??,Sarah Hopkins alias McCrady,Ezebel Hopkins alias
        Riggin, Martha Hopkins alias Porter,Jemima Hopkins alias
        Hurley
     wit;Samuel McClester,Samuel Townsend,William Harris,John.Harr
```

HANDY,Isaac   15 Jun 1772   23 Oct 1772
    to wife-Betty,dwelling plantation
    to sons-George(exec.),Joseph,Samuel,Thomas,Isaac, James
    to daus-Ann, Betty and Mary Handy
    George Day Scott to be gdn. of son Thomas (under 21)
    wit;George Day Scott,Thomas Dashiell,John Robertson

SCOTT,Windom   15 Mar 1772   4 Nov 1772
    to wife-Comfort,1/3rds. lands and house where I live
    to dau-Sarah Scott
    to son-Mitchell,plantation,exec.
    wit;Joseph Venables,John Roberson,Matthew Merine

ELLIS,Josias   4 Oct 1772   13 Oct 1772
    to son-Joseph Elllis
    to dau-Isbel Ellis
    brother-Stephen Ellis,exec.
    wit;James Hitch,Isaac Dashiell
    came-Rachel Ellis widow, demands 1/3rds.

END OF BOOK

BEVANS-Wm.-6
  Jennett-6
BIGLANDS-Mattux-128
  Richard-128
BLAIN-John-141
BLEWETT-BLUITT
  Eleanor-6-65
  Martha-6-65
BLURE-Joseph-62
  Margaret-62
BOND-Thomas-88
BOSTON-Betty-140
  Daniel-10
  David-10-83-140
  Elijah-140
  Esau-10-140
  Ephraim-140
  Isaac-10-140
  Jacob-140
  Martha-10
  Lazarus-10-140
  M ary-68
  Matthew-140
  Naboth-10
  Rachel-10
  Rebecca-10
  Richard-69
  Sarah-10
  Samuel-10
  Solomon-10-83
BOULDEN-Caleb-103
BOUNDS-BOWNES
  James-176
  Jonathan-144
  Mary-110
  Sarah-82
  Richard-52
BOWEN-Sarah-172
BOZMAN-Anne-6
  Bridget-6-65
  George-7-14-71
  Daniel-2
  Jane-2
  Levin-2
  Phillmon-2
  Sarah-14-71
  Susannah-2
BRADLEY-Richard-173
BREADY-Rebecca-101
  William-16
BRICKHOUSE-Abner-75
  John-75
BRITTINGHAM-Orpha-97
  Elizabeth-54
  Jessey-68
BROADWATER-James-53
BROUGHTON-Esther-38
  Jemima-38

BROUGHTON-John-38-60-131
  William-38-78
BROWN-Charles-59-90
  George-90
  James-64
  John-90-94
  Margaret-3
  Mary-88
  Robert-90
  Sarah-64
  William-60-64-94
BUCHANAN-Ann-143
  James-143
BUNCLE-BUNKOL
  Alexander-32
  John-65
BUNTING-Holloway-75
BURGIN-Mary-109
  Sarah-109
  William-109
BURRIDGE-Wm.-32
BURT-Deborah-156
  Elizabeth-156
  Joseph-156
  Margaret-156
  Richard-156
  Sarah-156
BUTLER-Elizabeth-98-136
  Nathaniel-98
BYRD-BIRD-Betty-59
  Benjamin-18-59-63-161
  David-64
  Catheron-59
  Elgat-59
  Joshua-59-172
  Mary-59
  Sarah-59
  Solomon-64
  Thomas-4-59-172

CALDWELL-John-119
  Mary-131
  Joshua-63
  Robert-63-131
  Rachel-65
  William-63-131
CALLOWAY-Aaron-67
  Ann-67-151
  Catherine-151
  Clammond-67
  Edward-151
  Ebenezer-151
  Elizabeth-61
  Isaac-151
  Joseph-128
  John-41-67-151
  Levi-151
  Matthew-61-67

CALLOWAY-Moses-61-67
  Rachel-151
  Sarah-151
  William-61-67
CANNON-Juda-13
  Matthew-135
CARMEAN-Moses-61
CARGLEY-Robert-83
CARMICAL-CARMICHAEL
  Rachel-50-74
  John-74
  William-74
CARREY-Ann-148
CARROW-John-91
CARRUTHERS-Wm.-5
CARTER-Samuel-127
CATLING-Ibby-12
  Fenton-12
CAVE-Anne-134
  John-134
  William-134
CEARSLY-Wm.-140
CEMEY-Elizabeth-26
CHAMBERS-John-126
CHENEY-Francis-58
  Andrew-87-131-172
CHITTAM-Francis-148
CHRISTOPHER-Hannah-54
  Clement-54-75
  Mary-54
  John-54-181
CLARK-James-11
CLARKSON-Fran-70
  James-70
CLIFTON-George-8
  Hannah-8-9
  John-8-9
  Jonthan-8
  Machel-8
CLOGG-Samuel-63
CLUFF-Edward-32-78
  Jonathan-46-60-78
  Michael-60-78-90-138
COHOON-Henry-159
COLLIER-Ann-56-101
  Betts-110-130
  Bridget-110
  Douty-56-101-110-123
  George-56-96-101-123-149
  Elizabeth-110
  Jean-123
  John-135
  Leah-110
  Luezar-110
  Nicholas-123-149
  Peter-32
  Priscilla-101-110-123-14
  Robert-56-81-101-110-130

DAVIS-Beauchamp-2
  Bridget-20-22-25
  John-9-25-81-95
  Mary-25
  Richard-25
  Sarah-20
  William-20-22-112
  123
DAWSON-John-5-23
DAY-Sarah-94
DEAN-Charles-106
  Ephraim-106
  George-57
  James-106
  Levie-106
  Noble-106
  Sarah-106
DENNIS-John-38-131
  Littleton-38-119-
  131-143-157
DENWOOD-Betty-53
  George-26
  John-53-86
  Levin-53-86
  Mary-26-30
  Thomas-26-30-183
DERBY-Walter-19
DERRIX-Peter-128
DICKESON-DICKERSON
  Cateron-179
  George-179
  Isaac-37-114-179
  Joshua-143-179
  James-179
  Levi-114-179
  Margaret-51
  Rachel-179
  Ruth-114-144
  Sarah-179
  Teague-114
  Peter-179
DIKES-James-119
DISHEROON-Elenor-51
  Bannister-51
  Constant-51-167-188
  Eunice-91
  Francis-70-167
  George-126-167-181
  Isbell-167
  Jlames-91
  John-51-70-91-188
  Jessee-91
  Joshua-91
  Josephus-51-167-188
  Levin-91
  Mary-51-91-167
  Nuton-167-188
  Obediah-70-167-188
  Margaret-91

DISHEROON-Michael-51-167
  Priscilla-91
  Stephen-167
  Thomas-167
  Weatman-91
  William-51-91
DIXON-Ambrose-1-7-14-71
  Elizabeth-7
  Isaac-1-132
  Nancy-180
  Risdon-1-7
  Sarah-1
  William-7-132
DOLBE-John-103
DONE-James-140
  John-15
DONOHO-Joshua-37
  William-49
DORMAN-Ann-24-126
  Betty-125
  Catherine-138
  Chase-157
  David-125
  Eleanor-126
  Elizabeth-126-157
  Hezekiah-52-126
  Isaian-157
  Jessee-147-157
  John-42-138-157
  Leah-50-125
  Major-18
  Matthias-138
  Mary-126-138-157
  Michael-157
  Matthew-74-82-125
  Nehemiah-88
  Sarah-125-126-152
  Solomon-157
  William-144
DOUGHERTY-DAUGHERTY
  Ezekiel-74
  Grace-74
  Isaac-74-80
  Jemima-74
  James-74
  John-74
  Leah-114
  Martha-74-80
  Nathaniel-74-130
  Obed-74
  Peter-74
  Rachel-74
  Sarah-74
  Stephen-74
DOWDLE-Nelly-74
  Christopher-25-54
  160
  Sarah-25-160
DOWNES-Robert-44

DRISKELL-Moses-59
DRYDEN-DREADEN
  Hamilton-141
  Jane-155
  Noble-78
  Jonathan-141
  Rachel-141
  Samuel-155
  Sewill-155
  Thomas-141
  William-12
DUSMUIR-Margaret-75
DUKES-Robert-8
DULANY-Dennis-161
  Henry-161
  John-161
  Mary-161
  Paul-161
DUNKIN-Catherine-174
  Easter-174
  Leah-174
  Margaret-174
DYES-Stephen-95

EDGE-Abigail-67
  Elizabeth-67
  Joshua-28-67
  Nehemiah-28-67
EDGILL-Wm.-8
ELGATE-Wm.-59
ELLEGOOD-Mary-106
ELLINGSWORTH-Ann-13
  Rachel-76
  Sarah-13
  William-109
ELLIOTT-Wm.-88
ELLIS-Isbel-192
  Joshua-154
  Joseph-192
  Josias-192
  Magdalene-154
  Rachel-192
  Stephen-100-192
ELZEY-Arnold-18-26
  Elizabeth-19
  James-18
  John-15-19-70-122
  Margaret-26
  Robert-19
  Sarah-19
ENGLAND-Jean-93
ENGLISH-James-116
  Cornelius-146
ENNELS-Col.-58
ESKRIDGE-Elizabeth-106
EVANS-Arrabella-64
  Ephraim-53-54
  Hannah-105
  John-64-75-96-105

59

EVANS-Leah-54-64
  Nathan-64
  Nathaniel-54
  Nicholas-96-105
  Rachel-64
  Richard-64
  Rebeccah-101
  Rease-54
  Solomon-64-75
  Thomas-54-64-75
  William-8-54
EVERTON-Thomas-24

FALLIS-Mary-13
FARRINGTON-Jane-50
  George-50-82-111
  Levin-50
  Robert-50-74
  William-50
FASSITT-Mary-81
FINCH-James-60
  John-60-70-99
  Margaret-60
FENTON-Esther-12
  Margaret-12
FINLEY-Rev.--88
FISHER-Rose-75
FITZWATERS-Ambrus-99
FLEMING-Jane-66
  John-95
  Sarah-95
  William-66
FLETCHER-Elizabeth-150
  George-150
  James-150
  John-150
  Thomas-150
  Levin-150
FLEULLING-Ann-118-124
  John-124
  Mary-124
  Rebecca-124
  Richard-124
  Samuel-124
FORDRED-Rebecca-130
  Wm.-7-39-71-83
FORTUNE-Betty=58
FOSCUE-Esther-172
FOUNTAIN-Collier-170
  Marcy-128
  Wm.-27-161-170
FRANSWAY-Benjamin-134
  Margaret-134
  Mary-134
FRAZIER-Ann-77
  William-152
FREENEY-Mary-43
FULLERTON-Alex.,-117
  Charles-117-155

FULLERTON-Leah-117
  James-117
  John-155
  Joshua-155
  Mary-117-155
  Peggy-155
  Tubman-117-155
FURNACE-FURNISS
  George-122
  James-122-125
  Jonathan-122
  Leah-45
  Priscilla-45
  Judith-122
  Sarah-122
  Wm.,-45-122

GALE-Col.-58
  Levin-88-119-127-
    128
  John-128
GARLAND-Stephen-73
  172
GASTINEAU-GASKENEW
  Elizabeth-139
  George-25-69-139
  Job-139
  Mary-139
  Matthew-90
GEDDIS-GEDDES
  Alexander-131
  John-15
  Robert-131
  William-131
GIBBONS-GIBBINS
  Ann-48-60
  Amey-90
  Elizabeth-48
  John-48-90
  Mary-48
  Robert-48
  Solomon-48
  Thomas-48-90
  William-48
GIBSON-John-87
GILES-Ann-148
  Isaac-60-148-174
  Jacob-146-148-174
  Sarah-148
  Thomas-8-148
  Wm.-8-23-148-174
GILLIS-Jane-17-44
  Joseph-3-109-187
  Levin-187
  Mary-187
  Sarah-187
  Thomas-41-187
GIVANS-Ann-9
  Day-9-82
  James-174

GIVANS-John-32
  William-9
GODDARD-Francis-112-151
  George-112
  John-112-161
  Sarah-112
GORDY-Eleanor-124
  Hannah-54
GOSLEE-GOSLING
  Ann-31
  Daniel-31
  Esther-31
  Joanna-31
  John-31
  Matthew-22
  Marah-31
  Priscilla-31
  William-31
GOUTE-Mary-95
GRAHAM-Ann-25
  Grissy-55-130
  John-55-114-130
  Mary-55
  Phillip-55-130
  Robert-55
GRAIR-Margaret-131
GRAVENOR-Thomas-99-184
  William-99-184
GRAY-Hannah-66
  William-47
GREEN-Abendengo-4
  Ezekiel-144
  George-18
  Isaac-144-168
  John-144
  Meshack-40
  Richard-40-113-144
  Samuel-144
GUIBERT-Susannah-157
GULLETT-George-46
GUNBY-James-81
GUPTON-Ann-118
  John-118

HACK-Peter-185
  Spencer-127
HALL-Ann-102
  Charles-154
  Jessee-179
  John-136
  Joshua-60-102-136
  Martha-119
  Richard-20-25
  Sarah-60
  Sary-165
  Thomas-102
  William-165
  Zorobable-102
HAMILTON-Elizabeth-131
  Sarah-30

60

HOPKINS-Jean-189
  Isaac-13-123-135-136
  Judey-5
  Izabella-59
  John-13-101-116-182
  Levi-13
  Matthew-119
  Mary-5
  Margaret-5
  Roger-56-101-116
  Robert-56-101-116-189
  Richard-189
  Sarah-5
  Steven-5-182-189
  Tabitha-5
  William-5
HORSEY-Elizabeth-81
  Isaac-14-81
  John-81-127
  Mary-7-81
  Outerbridge-132
  Revell-32-77-81-101-
  127
  Smith-14
  Stephen-16-81-161
  William-32-151
HOWARD-David-148
HUFFINGTON-HOFINGTON
  Betty-94
  Esther-94
  Lazarus-144
  Levin-184
  Margaret-94
  Mary-141
  Richard-94
  Thomas-94-184
HUGGINS-Ann-119
  Benjamin-119
  Hannah-18
  Mary-18
HUGHES-Elizabeth-128
HULL-Beauchamp-84
HUMPHRIS-Joshua-70-100
  Thomas-59-93-144-152
HURLEY-Jemima-189
HURST-Joseph-111
HUSK-Joseph-84
HUTCHENS-Elizabeth-24

IRVING-Betty-137
  Ann-17-44-137
  Eleanor-137
  George-17-44-110-134-
  137
  John-137
  Mary-137
  Thomas-110
  Sarah-44-110

JACKSON-Alse-110

JACKSON-Daniel-8
  Elihu-109
  George-109
  Henry-88
  John-109
  Joshua-56-109
  Mary-110
  Milla-110
  Samuel-22-109-
  144-174
  Sarah-22-109
  Surfiah-109
  William-109
JACOBS-Elizab.-136
JARVIS-Samuel-8
JENNER-John-88
JOHNSON-Benj.-20
  Elizabeth-20
  Joana-20
  John-8
  Mary-20
  Purnell-16-20-101
  Samuel-20
  Sarah-20
JONES-Ann-52-91-140
  Benjamin-3-21
  David-2
  Daniel-108-123
  Elizabeth-21-55-
  108-140
  George-21-98
  Isaac-67
  James-52-108-116
  John-3-21-29-52-
  140-157
  Jean-31
  Joshua-140
  Mary-29-126
  Margaret-52-140
  Phillip-108
  Prissy-126
  Phillemon-2
  Priscilla-44
  Robert-3-21-29-44-
  52-108-137
  Richard-140
  Sarah-52
  Thomas-3-21-29-44-
  84-73-140-185
  William-3-21-29-67
  Zekell-67
JORDAN-John-119
JUETT-Cateron-128
  John-128
  Leah-128
  Mary-128
  Nathaniel-128
  William-85-128
KARVIN-Matthew-93

KELLY-John-162
KEMP-Elender-174
  Matthew-174
KENNADY-Thomas-169
KENNERLY-Wm.,-93
KERR-Jacob-127
KILLAM-KELLUM
  Ann-156
  Edward-90-156
  Isbal-90
  John-62-90-111-156
  Mary-158
  Margaret-90-156
  Nicholas-156
  Priscilla-156
  Sarah-90-156
  William-156
KILLETT-KILLOTT
  Eunice-17
  Elizabeth-17
  Robert-128
KILSICK-Naomi-39
KING-Ann-32-162
  Benjamin-32-162
  Elizabeth-3-27
  Frances-127
  Ephraim-41-125-174
  Jessee-84-122-185
  Jenkins-127
  John=84-162-185
  Leah-162
  Levin-127
  Mary-32-127
  Nehemiah-32-118-127
  Robert-11-19-32-49-
  84-119-127
  Samuel-174
  Sarah-27-49
  Thomas-32-132
  Whittington-84-162
  Zorobable-127
KINNEY-Ann-153
  Joseph-153
  Mary-153
  William-153
KIRKPATRICK-David-9
KNIGHT-Elizabeth-173
  James-173
  Jonathan-181
  Mary-173
  Martha-173
  Tabitha-173
  Sarah-173
KNOWLES-Patience-154
  Richard-154

LANDEN-LAMBDEN
  Henry-24
  Thomas-68

LANDERS-Morgan-76
LANGCAKE-Cannon-70
  Francis-70
  Rachel-70
  Stephen-70
  Thomas-70
  William-70
LANKFORD LANGFORD
  Benjamin-40-83-150
  Edward-118
  Elijah-118
  Esther-118
  Joseph-30
  John-32-118-132
  Killiam-173
  Lazarus-95
  Mary-40
  Martha-92
  Judea-40
  Sarah-83
  Puzey-83
  Thomas-40-118-150
LARRAMER-Jane-76
LAWS-LAW
  Betty-145
  Eleanor-3
  Esther-62
  Gilbert-145
  James-62
  John-62-91-145-
    154-162
  Mary-71-14-156
  Nanney-145
  Panter-3-17-21-145
  Phillis-62
  Robert-3
  Sarah-62
  Thomas-145
  William-3-62-145
LAYFIELD-Betty-71
  Betsy-14
  George-126
  Jessee-126
  John-126
  Rebeccah-126
  Robert-126
  Solomon-126
  Thomas-178
LEATHERBURY-Betty-21
  Charles-21-26-42-
    47-108-123
  Ellinor-21-42
  Elizabeth-42
  John-21-32-42
Robert-42
  Sarah-32
  Thomas-21
LECATT-John-32
LEEK-Roda-128
LEONARD-Betty-124
  Benjamin-124

LEONARD-Jane-124
  John-124
  Joseph-124
  Nelly-124
  Nicholas-124
LINDOW-Rebeccah-26
LINSEY-LINDSEY
  David-186
  Francis-186
  Leah-186
  Priscilla-186
  Sarah-186
  Thomas-38-186
LISTER-Betty-66
  Jean-45
  Jessey-45-48-130
LLOYD-Betsy-119
  Edward-119
LONG-Asseneth-97
  Abigail-45
  Coulbourn-97-153
  David-45-185
  Elizabeth-185
  Easter-97
  Jean-48
  Jeffrey-10-48-97
    171
  John-119
  Josiah-45
  Littleton-45
  Mary-48-97
  Margaret-185
  Matilda-185
  Randolph-48
  Randal-135
  Rebeccah-185
  Samuel-48-134-171
  Saywell-97
  Sarah-48-97-134-
    185
  Solomon-185
  William-48-134-185
LORD-Henry-28-74
  Peter-80
  Sarah-28
LOW-LOWES
  Esther-24-87-128
  George-52-113-143
  Henry-17-65-69-86
    87-101-128
  Hudson-52-57-108-
    113
  John-52
  Rachel-52
  Ralph-113
  Robert-52
  Sarah-113
  Tubman-87-128

LUCAS-Margaret-128
LUMLEY-LUNBY-Unicy-174
  Benjamin-161
LYNCH-Mary-151
MACKEY-William-156
MACKLUER-Dolly-108
MACKMORIE-MACKMURRAY
  David-25
  King-49
  Nancy-135
  Rebecca-135-146
MACKNEIDER-Isabell-160
MACOME-John-32
MADDUX-Ann-136
  Alexander-46-60-133
  Bell-128
  Betty-133-136
  Daniel-133
  Elizabeth-102-133
  Ezekial-133
  Isaac-133
  Jenny-133
  Hezekiah-166
  Joseph-133
  John-102
  Leah-107
  Lazarus-102-136
  Mary-46-131
  Nelly-136
  Sarah-185
  Stoughten-136
  Thomas-38-102
  William-133
  Zacarias-133
  Zepheniah-133
MAGEE-John-116
  Magdalene--116
  Peter-116
  Thomas-22-116
MAGRATH-McGRATH
  David-13-15
  Esther-15
  Jane-15
  John-13
  Levin-13
  Mary-13
  Owen-13
  Robert-15
MALONE-MELONE
  Peter-157
  Robert-157
  William-148-157
MARRIDIKES-John-2
MARSHALL-Esme-75
  Isaac-140
  John-170
  Patience-75
  Neomi-11
  Thomas-10-75

MARTIN-Betty-162
  George-93
  Henry-117
  Elinor-172
  Isbal-117
  James-117
  Jonathan-71
  John-117-142
  Mary-117
  Nelly-117
  Robert-117
  Thomas-5-17-117
  William-117
MATTHEWS-Betty-78
  Boaz-129
  Benjamin-78
  David-78
  Elizabeth-78
  John-78
  Phillip=78
  Rebecca-78
  Samuel-103
  Sarah-78-129-145
  Tabitha-78
  Teague-78
MAUGHAN-Christopher-15
MEALY-Nelly-75
MEARS-Betty-75
  Ezekiel-75
  Dorothy-75
  John-75
  Robert-75
MELSON-Benjamin-25
  Samuel-25
MERINE-Charles-132
  Ester-132
  Jenitt--132
  John-132
  Matthew-190
  William-132
  Zorobable-132
MERRILL-Sarah-78
  Scarborough-78
MEZICK-MESSICK
  Ann-189
  Aaron-18-76-116-123
    182
  Covington-18-76
  Elihu-76
  Elizabeth-76
  Jacob-76-96
  Joshua-76
  James-76
  Tabitha-139
MILBOURN-Caleb-55-143
  Elijah-188
  Hannah-53
  Heziah-53

MILBOURN-Isaac-53
  Jacob-54-53-178
  John-55
  Joshua-53
  Lodowick-11-54-53
  Mary-53
  Matthew-53
  Nathan-53
  Ralph-11-20-37
    53
  William-53
MILES-Betty-128
  Betsey-46
  George-97
  Henry-77-81
  Matthias-157
  Rebeccah-77
  Samuel-77
  Stacey-48
  William-77-81-85
    101-106-114-158
MISTER-Hester-154
  Isbell-6
  Jonathan-6-9
  Moses-32-63-68
  Robert-6
  Smith-6
  Stacey-45
  Stephen-6
  William-6
  Comfort-64
MITCHELL-Betty-164
  Banester-127
  Isaac-11-30-127-
    164
  Irving-127
  Jane-164
  Jany-164
  James-164
  John-164
  Joshua-30-164
  Josiah-30-164
  Mary-30-75-163-
    164
  Priscilla-30
  Robert-30
  Stephan-30-163
  Thomas-76-185
MONTGOMERY-Thomas-95
MOOR-MOORE
  Ann-179
  Elizabeth-28
  Hannah-158
  Charles-28-169-179
  Isaac-71
  John-28
  Mary-100-113-176
  Rachel-77

MOORE-Risden-28
  Samuel-176
  Shiles-28-40
  Stephen-81
  Thomas-28-40-142-148-
    158-179
  William-28-40-142-
    165
MORGAN-Mary-93
  Joshua-93
MORRIS-Grace-54
  Isaac-119
MUNRO-Alexander-91
  Isaac-91
  Matthias-91
MURRAY-Abigail-11
  Phillip-12
  William-148

McCALEY-Patrick-173
McCLEMMY-Samuel-1
  Sarah-109
  William-3-27
  Whitty-3-109
McCLEMEY-Elizabeth-161
  Woney-161
McCLESTER-George-81
  John-58
  Joseph-3-62
  Neal-58-62
  Sarah-42
  Samuel-58-113-189
McCRADY-Sarah-189
McDANIEL-Ebey-94
  David-117
McDONALD-David-20
McINTIRE-Daniel-170
  Elizabeth-152
McKINTIER-Eliza-118
McLALLY-Patrick-60

NAIRNE-Eleanor-160
  Isabell-160
  James-55-160
  Robert-11
NEAL-John-91
  Margaret-91
  Mary-176
NELSON-Dinah-76
  Robert-119
  William-96
NEWMAN-Henry-62
  Isaac-62-109-157
  Martha-62
  Thomas-109-157
NICHOLAS-Betty-123
  Isaac-123
  Henry-123
  John-123

NICHOLAS-Roger-123
  Thomas-123
NICHOLSON-John-110
  Charles-88-147
  Joseph-110-135
  Mary-44-110-135
  Nancy-110
  Peggy-110-135
  Parthena-13
  Priscilla-110
  Risdon-154
NOBLE-Isaac-42
NUTTER-Hewitt-128
  Sarah-65
  William-52-84

OTLEY-OTTLEY
  Covinten-178
  James-11
  John-9
  Sarah-9-11
OUTTEN-Abram--159
  Purnell-10-79-92-
  128-129-137-140-
  159-179-186
  Shadrack-186
OUTTERBRIDGE-Wm.-81
  Sarah-56-101
OWENS-OWEN
  Mary-92-103
  Rachel-155
  Samuel-29

PARKER-John-84-140
PARKS-Arthur-75
  Job-75
  Tabitha-64
PARREMORE-John-25
  Abigail-112
  Benjamin-41
  Isaac-22-112
  James-112
  Joseph-41-146
  Joshua-84-112-131
  Mary-80
  Thomas-112-131
PARRIS-Sarah-54
PATERSON-Charles-147
  John-149
PEDEN-John-78
PERKINS-PURKINS
  John-38-46-60-90
  Mary-46-60-90
  Michael-46-60
  Sarah-46-60-90
  Thomas-60
  William-46-60-90

PERSONS-Robert-138
PHEBUS-John-142
  Martha-15
  Samuel-98
PHILLIPS-Alse-23
  Elizabeth-97
  Grace-97
  James-23-125-184
  John-23-97-176
  Josiah-174
  Margaret-52
  Richard-23-52-59
  Sarah-184
  Thomas-4-22
PIPER-Eleanor-65
  Christopher-65
  John-126-156
  Levin-187
  Leah-187
  Matthew-65
PITT-PITTS
  Jabez-54
  John-57
PLAVERRY-Dorkas-9
POLLETT-PULLOTT
  George-25
  Mary-131
  John-25
  Priscilla-25
  Sarah-25
  William-23-91-160
POLK-Ann-17
  David-17-22-123
  Josiah-131
  Joshua-160
  Mary-73
  Robert-17
POMEROY-Ralph-88
PORTER-Alex.,-125
  Daniel-146
  Francis-119
  Haist-146
  Hugh-113
  James-146
  MacCl.-113
  Martha-189
  Joshua-51-101
  Rebecca-146
  Sarah-146
POTTER-Betty-145
  Henry-92-145-159
  Mary-145
  Thomas-92-145
POWELL-Levi-107
  Levin-54-107
  Rachel-107

PRICE-Mary-108
PRIOR-PRYER-Ann-173
  David-137-173
  Randolph-173
PURNELL-Mary-1
  Levi-1
  Sarah-1
PUZEY-John-163
QUATTERMUS-Sarah-49

RAGLING-David-176
RAWLE-Benjamin-93
  Francis-93
  Joseph-93
RAWLINS-Charles-28
READ-REED-Esther-134
  Hezekiah-18-125-134
  James-18-134
  John-18-139
  Mary-18-172
  Margaret-18
  Moses-156
  Obediah-18
  Sarah-18-139
  Susannah-18
  Zachariah-18-125
READING-Elizabeth-53
REVILL-REAVILL-Bridget-98
  Charles-101
  Randall-151
REDDEN-Stephen-150
  William-150
REDDISH-Hiram-54
  John-117
  Nicholas-117
RELPH-George-146
  John-146
  Mitchell-41-146
  Rachel-146
  Sarah-146
  Thomas-146
  William-146
RENCHER-Baty-100
  Martha-26
  Mary-5
  Sarah-5
  Underwood-5
  William-5-119
RHOADS-Sarah-169
RICHARDSON-Benjamin-150
  Mary-175
  John-175
  Sarah-150
  Shadrack-135
RICKETS-Alexander-28
  Elizabeth-28

SUMMARS-John-71
  Joanna-71
  Jonathan-85
  Richard-71
SURMAN-SHURMAN
  Betty-168
  Edward-176
  Grace-75
  Isaac-176
  Joshua-176
  Leah-168
  Mary-168
  Nehemiah-168
  Sarah-152

TABB-Edmund-101
TALBARD-John-100
  Sarah-100
TATUM-John-138
  Elizabeth-138
TAWS-Keziah-80
TAYLOR-Elias-79
  Abraham-9-179
  Isaac-100-179
  James-134-100-179
  John-117-
  Mary-139-64
  Phillip-179
  P.-151
  Sarah-165-179
  Robert-83
  Willia-117
  William-9-138-179
TEAGUE-John-86
THOMPSON-THOMSON
  John-12-140
  Joseph-99
  William-127
THORNS-Sarah-105
TILMAN-TILGHMAN
  Aaron-32-122
  Elizabeth-125
  Gideon-46-138
  Elijah-48
  Elizabeth-125
  Isaiah-45-122-125
  Joseph-125
  Mary-125
  Margaret-48
  Nehemiah-138
  Sarah-125
  William-125
TILNEY-Hezekiah-75
TINDAL-Sarah-43
TOADVINE-Arnall-181
  Mary-181
  Stephen-181
  Thomas-51-181

TOMLINSON-
  Sayward-119
TOST-Ann-81
TOWNSEND-John-15
  Benjamin-15
  Joshua-15
  Mary-15-57
  Samuel-15-189
  Solomon-119
  Susannah-15
TRAHEARN-Ann-153-159
  Betty-153
  Cyrus-153-159
  Hannah-175
  Elizabeth-159
  James-26-153-175
  Samuel--153-173
TRAIN-Roger-74
TRAVIS-Elizabeth-98
TRUITT-John-177
  Solomon-18
TULL-Betty-154
  Charles-60
  Esther-154
  Handy-60
  John-14-91-102-110
    141-154
  Jonathan-103-164
  Joshua-154
  Levin-60
  Noble-6
  Rode-60-154
  Rachel-60
  Sarah-136
  Solomon-170
  Samuel-60-136
  Stephen-154
  Thomas-39-60-154
  William-60
TULLY-Joseph-84
  Wm.,-22-119-148
TURPIN-Betty-130-132
  Elizabeth-1-27
  Denwood-161
  Joshua-22-117-130
  John-130-161
  Mary-161
  Nehemiah-48-153-159
  Sarah-27
  Whitty-27-161-170
  Wm.-1-2-27-97-111-
    130-132-161-
TWILLEY-George-60
  Robert-52-117
  William-124
TYLOR-Thomas-64-75

VANCE-James-150

VAUGHN-Betty-169
  Ephraim-169
  James-169
  Jethro-169
  Jonathan-169
  Levin-169
  William-169
VENABLES-Joseph-184-190
  Joshua-63
  William-63-118
VINCENT-VINSON-Esther-93
  Benjamin-40-93
  George-93
  Isaac-18
  Jonathan-18
  James-18-40
  Joseph-40
  Jacob-40
  Matthias-18-161
  Sarah-18-40
  Thomas-16-18
WAGGAMEN-Capt.-55
  Elizabeth-13-88
  Henry-13-26-73-88
  George-88
  John-88
  John-88
  Mary-88
  Sarah-88
  William-88
WAILES-WALES
  Betty-146-179
  Daniel-12-49-55-130-137
  Elizabeth-49
  George-137-148
  Eunice-143
  John-137-143-146
  Joseph-49
  William-179
WAIT-Rachel-78
WALKER-Betty-139
  Charles-139
  Emmanuel-139
  Daniel-169
  Henry-139
  Jessee-139
  Mark-139
  Thomas-139
WALLACE-WALIS
  Easter-108
  Eleanor-3
  James-98
  John-3-49
  Joseph-98
  Leah-98
  Mary-98
  Matthew-87-98

WALLACE-Richard-98-108
  William-98
WALLER-Ann-113
  Ebenezer-166-181
  John-131
  Joshua-61
  Mary-131
  Richard-166
  Thomas-131
  William-145
WALSTOn-WALSTONE
  Boaz-94-151
  Jessee-94-151
  Joy-94-151
  John-94-151
  Rebecca- 94
  Thomas-32-162
  William-32-162
WALTER-Betty-139
  George-126-135
  Isabelle-139
  Robert-126-135
  John-15-62
  William-113-114
  Sarah-135
WARD-Alce-8
  Betty-85
  Benjamin-85
  Cornelius-97-38-71-
   110
  Isaac-85
  Jessee-158
  Joseph-80-85-110-
   142-185
  James-110-158
  Jacob-85
  John-74-80
  Jemima-85
  Kiziah-80
  Mathias-80
  Matthew-97
  Mary-71-80-85
  Rachel-158
  Starling-158
  Sarah-158
  Thomas-158
  Sabroah-8
  Samuel-80
  William-158
WARWICK-Elisha-188
  Martha-110-
  William-110
WATERS-Ann-87-128
  Abigail-32
  Dolly-24-86
  Edward-32-53-86-
   87-102-128
  Elizabeth-24-53-86
  109

WATERS-Esther-24-86
  George-53-86
  John-20-27-53-86
  Littleton-24-86-87
  Mary-86
  Richard-24-32-109
  Sarah-24-87-109
  Spencer-53-86
  Peter-86
  William-24-32-86
WATKINS-Mary-82
  John-82-117-155
WATSON-John-91
WATTS-Charity-106
WEATHERLY-Charles-84-111
  Constantine-111
  Elijah-50
  Ellenor-84
  Jane-13-15
  James-111
  John-50-84-111-156
  Joseph-50-84-111
  Jessee-84-111
  Joshua-111
  Mary-111
  Patience-111
  Samson-16
  Lotura-111
WEST-Abigail-4
  Betty-44
  Ezekiel-151
  James-4-127-141-176
  Sarah-141
WHARTON-Sophia-154
WHEATLY-Alice-77
  Ann-184
  Betty-90-177
  Esther-184
  James-184
  Mary-177
  Johnson-184
  Sampson-90-101-173-
   177
  William-81-158-177-
   184
WHEELDON-Benoi-58
WHITE-Betty-83
  Catheron-113
  Elias-83
  Stevens-83
  William-83-98
WHITAKER-Wm.-38
WHITE-Abigail-10
  Elias-54-63-102-164
  Elizabeth-91
  Isaac-179
  John-91
  Francis-91
  Sarah-159

WHITE-Thomas-159
  William-91
WHITHEAR-Rebekah-136
WHITTINGTON-Isaac-171
  177
  Joshua-74
  Mary-171
  Southy-171
  Stevenson-171
  William-171?
WILEY-Francis-57
  Martha-57
WILLIAMS-Arthur-7
  Benjamin-73
  David-132
  Elizabeth-7-73
  Charity-132-146
  Job-7
  John-7-8-22-41-73-
   112-116-132-61-93-146
  Jemima-7
  Josebeth-7
  Jacob-73-14
  Josiah-73
  Levin-72-132
  Mary-7-14
  Planner-132
  Priscilla-73
  Samuel-73
  Thomas-132-1
  William-7-30
WILLIN-Edward-96
  Elizabeth-152
  George-170
  John-2-152-170
  James-126-170
  Levin-152-170
  Leonard-152
  Littelton-152
  Matthias-170
  Priscilla-44-170
  Samuel 170
  Robert-152
  Thomas-101-118-152
   170
  William-118
WILLIS-Barnaby-27
  William-2
WILLS-Benjamin-154
  Isaac-154
  Lazarus-154
  Mary-154
  Sarah-154
WILSON-Ann-184-137
  Abigail-109
  Abraham-137
  Denwood-162
  David-64-134-137-162
  184

END OF BOOK

www.ingramcontent.com/pod-product-compliance
Lightning Source LLC
Chambersburg PA
CBHW031134020426
42333CB00012B/373